Tasmania
Clergy House
C. Bay.

8/-

ESSAYS IN LIBERALITY

ESSAYS IN
LIBERALITY

ALEC R. VIDLER

- 9351

SCM PRESS LTD
56 BLOOMSBURY STREET
LONDON

This volume first published 1957

Printed in Great Britain by The Camelot Press Ltd.,
London and Southampton

CONTENTS

5

PREFACE

FIVE of the ten essays in this volume were delivered as lectures on various occasions and have not hitherto appeared in print. The other essays, which are comparatively short, were originally contributed as articles to periodicals. What coherence the collection possesses derives from the fact that they are essays of a theologian who aspires after the liberality which is defined in the latter part of the first essay. He would not presume to say that he has already attained to it.

A. R. V.

King's College
Cambridge

I

CHRISTIANITY, LIBERALISM, AND LIBERALITY[1]

ACCORDING to the *New English Dictionary* the word 'Liberalism' was first used in 1819. I apprehend that it was not until the second quarter of the nineteenth century that its use became common. This is what John Morley said about it in his *Recollections*:[2]

> Alike with those who adore and those who detest it, the dominating force in the living mind of Europe for a long generation after the overthrow of the French monarchy in 1830 has been that marked way of looking at things, feeling them, handling them, judging main actors in them, for which, with a hundred kaleidoscopic turns, the accepted term is *Liberalism*.

And he continued:

> It is a summary term with many extensive applications; people are not always careful to sort them out, and they are by no means always bound to one another . . .
>   Respect for the dignity and worth of the individual is its root. It stands for pursuit of social good against class interest or dynastic interest. It stands for the subjection to human judgment of all claims of external authority, whether in an organized Church, or in more loosely gathered societies of believers, or in books held sacred.

Elsewhere, striking a single and somewhat different note,

[1] The C. J. Cadoux Memorial Lecture delivered at Yorkshire United Independent College, Bradford, on 3 May 1951, and repeated elsewhere on other occasions.

[2] Morley, *Recollections* (1921 ed.), i. 18f.

which I shall pick up presently, Morley said: 'Define it as we may, faith in Progress has been the mainspring of Liberalism in all its schools and branches.'[1]

There we have the testimony of a professed friend and adherent of Liberalism. Let us set beside it the view of an equally eminent opponent, the accuracy of whose specification was, by the way, conceded by Morley.[2] John Henry Newman, in the address he gave in 1879 when he was made a Cardinal, alluded to the fact that for fifty years he had resisted to the best of his powers the spirit of Liberalism in religion. And he proceeded to define it in the following paragraph:

> Liberalism in religion is the doctrine that there is no positive truth in religion, but that one creed is as good as another. . . . It is inconsistent with any recognition of any religion as *true*. It teaches that all are to be tolerated, for all are matters of opinion. Revealed religion is not a truth, but a sentiment or a taste; not an objective fact, not miraculous; and it is the right of each individual to make it say just what strikes his fancy. Devotion is not necessarily founded on faith. Men may go to Protestant Churches and to Catholic, may get good from both and belong to neither. They may fraternise together in spiritual thoughts and feelings, without having any views at all of doctrines in common, or seeing the need of them. Since, then, religion is so personal a peculiarity and so private a possession, we must of necessity ignore it in the intercourse of man with man. If a man puts on a new religion every morning, what is that to you? It is as impertinent to think about a man's religion as about his sources of income or his management of his family. Religion is in no sense the bond of society.[3]

It would be difficult to deny that that describes very well the

[1] 'Liberalism and Reaction' in *Oracles on Man and Government* (1921 ed.), p. 101.

[2] See *Recollections*, i. 20.

[3] See Wilfrid Ward, *The Life of John Henry Cardinal Newman* (1913), ii. 460.

attitude to religion that has been prevalent in modern England. It has certainly been the attitude of the man in the street, and it has eaten more or less deeply into the mentality of all of us, including those who may now violently repudiate it. These commonly denounce some of the secondary manifestations of Liberalism rather than its basic principle.

For Newman might have added that the principle of Liberalism in religion is *laissez faire*. The once famous or notorious Dr R. D. Hampden, who was the Aunt Sally of the Oxford Movement of the eighteen-thirties, defined it when he spoke of 'the great principle . . . of leaving the course of nature as much as possible to its own free action, instead of encumbering and impeding it by officious regulations'.[1] 'It is an universal maxim', said Joseph Priestley, 'that the more liberty is given to everything which is in a state of growth, the more perfect will it become.'[2] Stephen Gwynn has spoken of 'the typical Liberal—the man who believes in leaving human nature to regulate itself according to its native virtue'.[3] Those who seek economic causes for social and cultural changes will not fail to observe that the vogue of Liberalism in politics and in religion followed on the period of *laissez faire* in economics, and that today it has its liveliest champions in those countries where collectivism and planning have been slowest to supervene on *laissez faire* politics.

We may be sure that there is more than mere coincidence in the concurrence of political and religious Liberalism with *laissez faire* economics, but it would be a very partial and incomplete account which treated and dismissed the one as no more than a concomitant of the other. To the progressive

[1] See Henrietta Hampden, *Some Memorials of Renn Dickson Hampden, Bishop of Hereford* (1871), p. 47.

[2] Quoted by B. Willey, *The Eighteenth Century Background* (1940), p. 199.

[3] See his introduction to F. S. Oliver's *The Anvil of War* (1936), p. 16.

English minds of the nineteenth century it seemed that every department of life was encumbered with, and impeded by, officious regulations. The old order in Church and State was obsolete but still powerful. It was exhilarating work challenging privilege and striving for emancipation—the emancipation of slaves abroad, of Romish and Protestant dissenters at home, of the middle classes, of the proletariat, of the Irish, and finally of women. The extension both of the franchise and of education appeared in this liberating light.

In every direction there were traditional shackles to be removed, and moribund ideas to be exploded. New philosophies and new scientific discoveries kept on pouring in to stimulate the process. Everywhere there was a release from old prejudices and restraints, and a revolt against cramping creeds and dull customs. By and large, the Liberals were those who were on the side of the new forces and the emancipating movements. In the early days they derived additional exhilaration from being an unpopular minority and from being persecuted. What is more exciting, it has been justly asked, 'than pursuing a reforming mission among those who see themselves as the greatest reforming missionaries of all time'?[1] The Liberals attracted to themselves the most active and independent minds. Their confidence was extraordinary. It seemed to them that their cause was irresistible. 'Progress', said Herbert Spencer, 'is not an accident, but a necessity. Surely must evil and immorality disappear; surely must man become perfect.'[2] 'We grow to good', declared George Meredith, 'as surely as the plant grows to light.'[3] 'The great social forces', said Gladstone,

[1] Douglas Hyde, *I Believed* (1950), p. 34.

[2] Herbert Spencer, *Social Statics* (1892 ed.), p. 32. See the whole passage. In an additional note to this edition Spencer said he would wish to qualify what he had written forty years earlier about the rate of progress.

[3] *Letters of George Meredith* (1912), i. 237; cp. ibid., ii. 497.

'which move onwards in their might and majesty are marshalled on our side.'[1]

Those may be extreme specimens of Liberal rhetoric. Men were affected by the climate of the age in different degrees, or drank of its spirit in different sized glasses. A man might be Liberal in one sense or in one sphere and Conservative in another. This indeed was the case with Herbert Spencer himself, who was the doyen of philosophic Liberalism, but eventually turned Conservative in politics—and Gladstone too, whose philosophy and theology were fundamentally traditionalist, but who was accepted as the leader of political Liberalism. So infectious was the confidence of the Liberals in progress that even the anti-Liberals caught it. So we find Spurgeon declaring: 'Every century sees a marked advance in the world's condition, and we shall proceed at a quicker rate when the Church wakes up to her responsibility.'[2] Even Newman, who was anti-Liberal *par excellence*, was regarded, not without some warrant, as a 'Liberal Catholic'.

It seems that the one thing that all those who professed to be, or who were labelled as, Liberals had in common was a concern for more freedom from constraint, and therefore Liberalism presupposed the existence of things or the operation of forces that you wanted to be rid of, or of established institutions that you wanted to make more flexible, so that man's native virtue might be released. It might be economic, or political, or speculative, freedom that was demanded. It might be freedom from legal restraints, from the dead hand of the past, or from vested interests of one kind or another, aristocratic, academic, ecclesiastical. It might be freedom to engage in novel experiments, or fresh ways of thinking, or unusual

---

[1] The words are engraved on the pedestal of a silver statuette of Gladstone making a speech, which is at St Deiniol's Library, Hawarden.

[2] C. H. Spurgeon, Sermon No. 1717 (1883).

conduct. Still, on the whole it was liberty *from*, rather than liberty *for*, which was the hall-mark of, or at any rate the uniting factor in, Liberal endeavour. Liberalism, it may be remarked, was not characteristically concerned with that kind of liberty of which Thomas Erskine of Linlathen said: 'True liberty consists in being delivered from our own vain passions and appetites and selfish will.'[1]

Now it is clear that men might want one or more of the external freedoms, and for quite different reasons or from quite different motives. This makes all generalization on the subject difficult, or it means that the term 'Liberalism' covers a heterogeneous collection of ideas. But with that proviso, if we were to assign a governing idea to Liberalism it would be that men are naturally good and reasonable, and that if you leave the course, not perhaps of nature but, of human nature as much as possible to its own free action, all will be for the best in the best of all possible worlds. It may be hard to believe now that men of great intelligence entertained and were sustained by this belief, but those of us who can imaginatively cast ourselves back into the heyday of England in the nineteenth century will be able to feel something of its intoxication, and in the U.S.A. they do not have to cast themselves back quite so far as that. It is important to remember that the Victorian Liberals, whether Christian or otherwise, belonged, as someone has said, to the happiest class of the happiest country in the happiest period of the world. The Liberal idea was certainly much more plausible then and in those circumstances than it can possibly seem to us today who contemplate the sorry remnants of it, which we may still sometimes display in our shop window but which are certainly no good for export.

We should however be doing many of the eminent Liberal statesmen, divines and men of letters in the nineteenth century

[1] See William Hanna, *Letters of Thomas Erskine of Linlathen* (1878), p. 378.

a grave injustice if we supposed that they really held such simple and sanguine opinions about the perfectibility of human nature and the inevitability of human progress as became associated with Liberalism in its decline. The young men, and not only the young men, who now airily attribute to them such simplicity and credulity, should read Mill and Morley and the rest. Nearly all the Victorian Liberals had been nurtured in the Christian tradition, and its sombre realism had left an imprint on their imaginations; and this imprint, however much they turned their backs on it or modified their profession of orthodoxy, continued to influence their outlook on the world. And they sometimes confessed to having a nostalgia for the past. 'Oh, that we were in those old ages of noble, grave belief!' Morley once wrote to Frederic Harrison.[1] It was Morley too, perhaps the greatest and purest Liberal of them all, who, when the Countess of Aberdeen suggested that he need not come to family prayers, made the admirable reply that he would certainly come down if only to renew his own sense of littleness amid the mysteries of life, and to begin the day with a feeling of fellowship in service with the humblest members of the household.[2] Most of those who became agnostics were profound and active agnostics. They took the metaphysical questions seriously. See the proceedings of the Metaphysical Society, where Huxley and Tyndall, Morley and Leslie Stephen, rubbed shoulders with Gladstone and Manning,

---

[1] F. W. Knickerbocker, *Free Minds: John Morley and his friends* (1943), p. 38. Cp. Morley's criticism of Voltaire, e.g. *Voltaire*, pp. 222f. Of Morley A. G. Gardiner wrote (*Prophets, Priests, and Kings*, 1914 ed., p. 150): 'His reflection upon life is touched with an abiding melancholy which differentiates him from his masters, who saw in the triumph of reason and logic the solution of all the problems of society. He cultivates no such confident optimism, but seems to detect in modern life the odour of decay, to see our civilisation not lit by the auroral light and bursting to perfect and enduring forms, but passing into the twilight whither the gods have vanished.'

[2] Knickerbocker, op. cit., p. 69.

James Martineau and F. D. Maurice. To borrow what Morley said of Voltaire 'if they were unflinching against theology they always paid religion respect enough to treat it as the most important of all subjects.'[1] Is there a comparable metaphysical seriousness among our eminent men today, even in universities?

As regards the Christian Liberals or the Broad Church—similar considerations apply. And it is time that we turned our attention to them. Whatever might happen to the top of their minds, however much they were allured by the spirit of the age, there remained a substantial residuum of Christian belief in the bottom of their hearts. The following, scarcely sympathetic, description, by a Belgian Jesuit, of nineteenth-century Liberal Christianity has no doubt its pertinence to the English Liberal divines of the period, but it is much less just as a description of Liberal theology in England than on the continent.

They spoke no longer of redemption but of civilization; no longer of salvation but of culture; no longer of sin but ignorance; no longer of heaven but of progress; no longer of the Church but of humanity; no longer of the Creed but of Science; no longer of eternity but of the future. . . . One no longer discussed miracle, one passed over it, as one passed over the Old Testament, the obscure promises to the Jews, and nine-tenths of the Gospel. Suffering was only a false note. One contrived to reduce it, or—who knows?—perhaps one day to eliminate it scientifically. Man as such was no longer for himself a tragedy; and God having ceased to be embarrassing was no more than a majestic decoration. The whole nineteenth century lived with this idea—however preposterous it seems—that man was going by his own efforts alone to make the earth a heaven and himself an embodiment of wisdom.[2]

[1] See Morley, *Voltaire*, p. 7.

[2] Pierre Charles, S.J., art. 'Réflexions sur la théologie du sermon' in *Nouvelle Revue Théologique* (June 1947), p. 592. Cp. a paragraph by Reinhold Niebuhr, quoted in C. W. Kegley and R. W. Bretall, *Reinhold Niebuhr: his religious, social, and political thought* (1956), p. 196.

That is less than just, I say, to the English Liberal divines. Benjamin Jowett, wrote one of his biographers, 'was profoundly attached to Christianity, which had penetrated to the very core of his nature; to the Bible, which he desired to see made the rule of life, not in the letter, but in the spirit; and to the Church of England, whose ministry seemed likely to be impoverished by the unrealities of popular theology'.[1] Yet J. B. Mozley also had good ground for remarking in his sardonic manner: 'If the letter of Scripture is a veil, and Christianity is Jowett behind the veil, one does not feel very secure.'[2]

The truth is that the intellectual forte of the Liberal divines was criticism, negation, opening up new questions. And all these things needed to be done. Traditional orthodoxy needed to be thoroughly criticized; there was much in it that required to be simply negated; there were endless questions that were due to be opened up. The Liberal divines did these things to the best of their ability, and were exposed to a cross-fire for their pains. In the event they secured liberty of thought and speech and publication in the Church of England, and in most of the Reformed Churches, and even at odd moments in the Church of Rome. They secured the condition of a flexibility that was necessary if a new reformation was to be set in motion. And many who now take advantage of this flexibility omit to acknowledge, or perhaps are unaware, of their debt to those who won it for them. But as for the constructive work of a new reformation, the Liberal divines left almost everything to be done, and it has yet to be done. The Liberal Protestant was in his

[1] Abbott and Campbell, *Life and Letters of Benjamin Jowett* (1897), i. 260. Cp. John Bennett in *Union Seminary Quarterly Review*, November 1951, p. 3: 'There is a danger of caricaturing individual thinkers of an earlier period by attributing to them certain general tendencies that we discern as characteristic of their period without allowing for the fact that many of them were dependent upon the Bible and the Christian tradition as well as upon the thought of the period.'

[2] *Letters of the Rev. J. B. Mozley* (1885), p. 245.

element when debunking biblical fundamentalism; the Liberal Catholic when exploding claims to ecclesiastical infallibility; but their own essays in reconstruction were hardly less vulnerable intellectually, and were less spiritually substantial, than the systems from which they sought emancipation. In other words the Liberal divine is in his element when he is deflating obscurantism and tripping up blind guides; when he is standing for freedom from the pretensions of an intransigent or corrupt authority. But when all authority has been laid low, including the ultimate authority which can alone give freedom its sanction and responsibility, 'now the day is over' for the Liberal and 'night is drawing nigh'. It is not his *métier* to restore or to vindicate authority. It is no longer his turn. Of course he can go on polishing his critical apparatus and driving home his shafts, and he may be doing some good, for as long as the world lasts there will be obscurantism that needs to be deflated and bogus authoritarianism that needs to be exposed.

But that is not the main need in the twentieth century, and that is why the prospects both of Liberalism and of Liberal divinity look very different now from what they did at the turn of the century. That is why Christian Liberals, where they survive, are today plaintive and querulous and defensive, where they used to be confident and bold and aggressive. Freedom to believe and say what you think has been won; nobody minds what you believe or say; we are no longer shocked. In such a world the Liberal has lost his bearings. Original and independent minds are no longer attracted to his ranks. For Liberalism has ceased to be original. We can be as independent as we please. The question now is whether there is any authority or Law or God in the world and over the world, on which we can depend, in which we can trust, to whom we are responsible, whom we can know and love—whether we belong to a race that is damned and left to itself, or to a race

18

that has been redeemed, reconciled and united in a Head from on high.

Historians of the Oxford Movement in the Church of England are fond of quoting Dr Arnold's dictum, 'The Church, as it now stands, no human power can save', as though subsequent history had refuted it. But the saying was true then and it is true now. The nineteenth century revivals—Evangelical, Catholic and Liberal—have spent their force. The state of English Christianity is on the whole well indicated in some words written by Erich Meissner:

> Religions . . . can go on existing after they have ceased to function. The doctrine is still taught and—so it seems—accepted; the rites, the customs, the ceremonies, the paraphernalia remain. There seems hardly any change at all, but the old words and terms sound hollow; dullness creeps in and takes the lustre away from things that once stirred and invigorated the hearts of men.[1]

Nor is that merely the verdict of a detached intellectual. Here is a recent comment on a Mass Observation survey in Britain:

> Religion . . . has, in the minds of the great majority, become simply irrelevant to the question of living. It seems to have no connection with life, and no relation to the real day-to-day problems of modern society. What has been rightly described as 'a sort of inert agnosticism' seems to have settled on people's minds and the vitality of religious belief has quietly evaporated.[2]

When or where renewal will arise—or descend—we cannot tell. We can however observe that something that looks like the beginnings of renewal has already come to churches on the continent which have been exposed to trials and purgations from which Anglo-Saxon Christianity has so far been exempt. There, lustre has been coming back to the old symbols and

---

[1] Erich Meissner, *Germany in Peril* (1942), p. 37.
[2] See *The Tablet*, 26 July 1947, p. 54.

myths and dogmas. Nevertheless, it is as yet uncertain whether this is the swan-song of Christianity on the European continent or the signal of its coming rejuvenation. The future of Europe is dark at every level; or if we may speak of a twilight, it looks at least as much like the twilight that precedes the night as that which precedes the dawn. Anyhow, it is notorious that Anglo-Saxon Christians, who are still living in the late afterglow of Liberalism, find themselves ill at ease in that foreign atmosphere. Some indeed of our divines have been trying to imitate or to imbibe or to acclimatize theological reactions which were spontaneous and genuine on the continent, but which seem somewhat artificial or self-conscious or secondhand with us, because the conditions have hardly yet arisen to which they correspond or which call for them. We have no doubt in Britain some profound, if obscure, diagnosticians of our own disease, but no voice has yet been uplifted that has the note of authentic and inspired prophecy. For myself, I confess that, so far as Britain is concerned, I hear that note more clearly in F. D. Maurice and P. T. Forsyth, theologians who delivered their word in the spring and autumn of the Liberal period, than in any contemporary Christian spokesmen.

The Liberal divines at their best are too sophisticated, too urbane, too tolerant, and too sweetly reasonable, to constitute a social stratum from which a fundamental renewal of Christianity, or of anything else, is likely to proceed. As Ernest Troeltsch said: 'The really creative, church-forming, religious movements are the work of the lower strata. Here only can one find that union of unimpaired imagination, simplicity in emotional life, unreflective character of thought, spontaneity of energy and vehement force of need, out of which an unconditioned faith in a divine revelation, the *naïveté* of complete surrender, and the intransigence of certitude can arise.'[1] It is not

[1] Quoted by W. L. Sperry, *Religion in America* (1945), p. 96.

yet possible to say from what lower strata in contemporary society such a new spring of life might come. Some whose opinion I respect think that this very good thing may come from the other side of the Iron Curtain. Nor in this connexion can we forget the apostolic quality of life in some of the younger churches. Of this we can only say that the Spirit bloweth where it listeth, but it will be astonishing indeed if it blows a renewal of Christianity and of civilization out of Liberal divinity.

What then should we say of the prospects of 'Christian Liberalism'? Men may of course define words as they please. But I suggest that the term 'Liberalism' should be kept for the nineteenth-century phenomenon which Morley espoused and Newman attacked, but which they were sufficiently agreed in defining. Liberalism, which flowered in the nineteenth century, has run to seed in the twentieth. Much of the seed, though not, or not yet, in Britain, has produced dragon's teeth. In Britain it has left us with a confused crop of rather sickly tares and wheat. But while Liberalism, whether Christian or otherwise, can be dated and dated without compunction, this is by no means the case with the virtues, the temper and the cast of mind that I would use the epithet 'liberal' (with a small 'l') to denote, with liberality as its substantive. These qualities are much older than Liberalism. They have their roots in classical antiquity. They are as old as a liberal education.

Here the word 'liberal' denotes not a creed or a set of philosophical assumptions or any 'ism, but a frame of mind, a quality of character, which it is easier no doubt to discern than to define. A liberal-minded man is free from narrow prejudice, generous in his judgment of others, open-minded, especially to the reception of new ideas or proposals for reform. Liberal is the opposite not of conservative, but of fanatical or bigoted or intransigent. It points to the *esprit large* and away from the *idée fixe*. The liberal temper or frame of mind is not common and perhaps is never likely to be. It can be preserved, even by those who have once possessed it, only by constant vigilance and exercise. For most men's minds and ideas tend to become set and inflexible as they grow old, indeed as they grow middle-aged—and sometimes while they are still young —and it is as rare as it is delightful to find an old man who possesses a mature wisdom and at the same time can really receive new ideas and sympathize with them, play with them and work with them. The liberal frame of mind does not appear to be more common among the adherents of Liberalism, or other 'isms that are ostensibly progressive, than among the adherents of systems that are professedly conservative. Morley acknowledged that this was so. 'The vanity and egoism of rationalistic sects', he said, 'can be as fatal to candour justice and compassion as the intolerant pride of great churches.'[1] For it is the law of systems of thought and of sets of ideas, of sects and parties, whatever their original aim, to harden and become inflexible, and so for their vitality to ebb. 'In its prime', said Whitehead, 'every system is a triumphant success; in its decay it is an obstinate nuisance.'[2] Thus every 'ism that was once a spur, becomes in the end an obstacle, to movement.

The liberal temper is not peculiarly Christian, though the Christian man, wherever he finds it, will acknowledge God as its author. Ancient Greece and China would confute any claim on the part of Christians to have a monopoly of it. It may be described as one of the natural virtues, provided that by the word 'natural' we do not intend to exclude the Holy Spirit from originating and inspiring it. It is a virture which the gospel ought to affirm and deepen and perfect. But we must

[1] Morley, *Rousseau*, ii. 82.
[2] Quoted by S. A. Cook, *The 'Truth' of the Bible* (1938), p. 129.

admit that in some periods the conditions within and without the Church are more favourable than in others to its cultivation. In the Old Testament it is more in evidence in the Wisdom literature than in the prophets. The liberal temper is not as conspicuous in the New Testament (though we know how much people succeed in reading into that) as in the Greek Apologists or as in Clement of Alexandria and Origen. Yet without the publication of the gospel of the New Covenant the later men could not have done their own special work. It would seem that great truths have first to be boldly and provocatively proclaimed, in a raw and rugged manner, and that only afterwards comes the time for analyzing, qualifying, refining and systematizing them. It is at this latter stage that men of liberal temper can do their best work. It is then that their prospects are brightest and their accomplishments are most appreciated.

Perhaps it was the tragedy of the Reformation, which was at first another proclamation of great truths and a release of new forces, that those who followed on and consolidated the work of the original Reformers were not men of liberal temper but (with rare exceptions like the judicious Hooker) hard and fanatical systematizers. Thus Christian theology lost its flexibility and vitality in the arid marshes of Catholic and Protestant scholasticism, and though it may have recovered its flexibility it has hardly yet renewed its vitality.

A rejuvenation of theology is not likely to be brought about by the intellectual refinement in which liberal divines excel. What is needed now is a profound and revolutionary rediscovery of theological truth, which is likely to be very *un*refined in its first manifestations. Perhaps God in the pulpit of history is about to utter, indeed has for some time been uttering, some crude words. These words are as shocking to the liberal temper as to every other. While the liberal-minded may at first be the most nonplussed, there will nevertheless, if history continues, be work ahead for them to do, and for which they can already be preparing.

There is in fact plenty to be done. All Christians ought to be opening their minds more widely and deeply to the revelation of the living God to which the Bible bears witness, and nature and history too in their own ambiguous ways. It ought at present to be the particular task of liberal divines to be getting under the skin of the Marxists and the Freudians and the linguistic philosophers, and to be treading the dark night of the intellect which awaits those who go deeply into the relativity and sociology of knowledge. For the minds to which the rediscovered gospel will have to be commended will have been shaped or confounded by such disciplines and scepticisms as these. I do not know what Christians there are yet in Britain who are on the way to being qualified to communicate with such minds.

Professor H. A. Hodges has finely said: 'In the face of error, as in face of evil, the Christian has a choice of two types of strategy. The first is that of firm resistance, stone-walling as it might be called, meeting every move of his opponent with a steady denial, and a steady reassertion of the principles to which he is himself committed. . . . It fights the enemy to a standstill, but it does not convert him.' I interject that that is broadly speaking, the strategy of the Vatican, and its effectiveness and impressiveness should not be underestimated. 'The second type of strategy [continues Hodges] is that of comprehension, which enters into the mind of the enemy and transcends him from within. The Christian here is not the soldier of pure truth in conflict with the servant of the lie. He stands side by side with his opponent, sinner with sinner, under the judgment of God which condemns and transforms them both. He carries his opponent with him into the Presence, and shares with him both the inevitable death and the promised resurrection. To let down our barriers, to enter into the heart of the modern intellectual situation, to undergo in ourselves something of what the Christless world perpetually endures, and in the midst of the storm to invoke Him who commands the wind and the waves on behalf of those who do not know His name—this is not easy, but it is the only way of redemption. It is the way of the cross, and, indeed, there is an intellectual as well as a moral and a spiritual cross to be borne.'[1]

Finally, we may say that the perennial office of the liberal in the Church and in society is to be critical and astringently so; critical of prevalent moods and popular fashions and hidden assumptions and powerful cliques, and not least of himself and his friends. He must be *impartial* in his criticism, which is to say that the formation of a liberal party in the Church is a double contradiction in terms. Liberals will always be in a minority. Their role is a subordinate, but a salutary, an antiseptic or aperient, one. While they have their own peculiar temptations to pride, yet if they do their work well they will keep the Church humble. Archbishop Whately of Dublin was a good liberal when he said that he was 'even more mortified by weak arguments in favour of his own views than by strong ones against them'.[2] And so was Principal Denney when he said that 'if one lectured for a session without leaving a deep impression of ignorance, it would be the most pitiable of all failures'.[3] So again was Dr Figgis who was once out for a walk at Cambridge with Dr Barnes, the late Bishop of Birmingham: when Barnes turned to Figgis at a certain point and said, 'The trouble with you, Figgis, is that you don't get to the

---

[1] Essay on 'The Crisis in Philosophy' in *Reformation Old and New*, ed. by F. W. Camfield (1947), p. 194.

[2] E. Jane Whately, *Life and Correspondence of Richard Whately* (1866), ii. 28.

[3] James Denney, *Letters to His Family and Friends*, ed. by J. Moffatt, p. 74.

bottom of things,' Figgis replied, 'Barnes, there is no bottom.'[1]
And Walter Bagehot's words about Clough are a tribute to a
liberal mind: 'He saw what it is considered cynical to see—
the absurdities of many persons, the pomposities of many
creeds, the splendid zeal with which missionaries rush on to
teach what they do not know; the wonderful earnestness with
which the most incomplete solutions of the universe are thrust
upon us as complete and satisfying.'[2]

The liberal vocation, faithfully exercised, is not only
humbling but also reconciling. It has the effect of showing that
no party or school of thought or phase of orthodoxy is ever as
right as its protagonists are inclined to suppose, and that men,
including Christian men, have much more in common both of
frailty and strength, both of falsehood and truth, than the
makers of systems and sects acknowledge. But great works of
construction will not be done, so far as we can see, by liberals
as such, nor great decisions taken. So far it has been the
Luthers and not the Erasmuses who have changed the course
of history. As F. S. Oliver said in his Life of Alexander
Hamilton: 'In the supreme events, it is not sufficient to be reasonably persuaded; the man who is to succeed must be unreasonably confident.'[3] But the liberal *ex officio* is *not* unreasonably
confident.

That, I suppose, is why great preachers have seldom been
characterized by the liberal virtues. Liberality is not what most
men look for nor what they need in preaching. 'Assertions,
hesitatingly expressed or qualified with modest reserve, may
suit the lecture-room or the study, but they are out of place
in the pulpit. An eager, heavy-laden soul crying out from his
heart, "What must I do to be saved?" will listen only to a

---

[1] See M. G. Tucker, *J. N. Figgis* (1950), p. 55.
[2] See W. Ward, *Ten Personal Studies* (1908), p. 91.
[3] Op. cit. (1928), p. 412.

preacher who shows that he believes himself with all his energy in the answer that he gives.'[1] Nor are liberals usually pioneers in the propagation of the gospel. P. T. Forsyth called attention to the fact that the great Protestant missions of the last hundred and fifty years, which have spread light and healing round the world, 'did not arise out of the liberal thinkers, the humanitarian philosophers of the day, who were its worst enemies, but with a few men—Carey, Marshman, Ward and the like—whose Calvinistic theology we should now consider very narrow'.[2]

It would appear then that in the economy of the Church there is need for both types—the unreasonably confident and the astringently sceptical; both have their indispensable contribution to make to the mission and message of a church. Hitherto they have been separate and even rival types. I should like to raise the question whether they need always be so; the question is whether we shall always have to choose between Luther and Erasmus. May it not be that it is within the resources of the Holy Ghost to knit together in the same persons both apostleship and liberality—both the unshakeable conviction of the prophet and the cleansing scepticism of the wise man? Perhaps a German theological student was on the right track who was reported as having said: 'We must try to be at one and the same time *for* the Church and *against* the Church. They alone can serve her faithfully whose consciences are continually exercised as to whether they ought not, for Christ's sake, to leave her.'

May it not be that a new reformation will issue in a new type of Christian character, of which the New Testament contains some hints and the kalendar of saints, canonized and uncanonized, some signs of promise? We have yet to see—but

---

[1] J. A. Froude, *Short Studies in Great Subjects*, iii. 138.
[2] P. T. Forsyth, *The Work of Christ* (1938 ed.), pp. 61f.

may we not hope to see?—held up to Christendom as a pattern of holiness and to theologians as their patron saint—the man who is tolerant, not because he regards all opinions as doubtful, but because he knows that God alone is true,—the man who is ready to learn from all men, not because he has no creed of his own, but because his creed assures him that God is teaching and chastening all men,—the man who has plumbed the meaning for the human intellect of the great New Testament word about having nothing and yet possessing all things,—the man who can at once rigorously doubt and sincerely believe,—in short the man who has discovered that it is not only the sinner but the doubter who is justified by faith.

II

THE FUTURE OF THEOLOGY[1]

ONE day during the 1930s when a Cambridge theologian was walking by the Divinity School— the headquarters of the theological faculty in the university—he was passed by an anthropologist and a psychologist walking in the opposite direction. As they passed, the theologian heard the anthropologist say to the psychologist: 'You know, within fifty years we shall be in there.' It is a parable of what then seemed possible, and indeed is still possible, though there are as yet no evident signs that the existence of theological faculties is coming to be attacked as an archaism.

When the ancient universities were preserves of the Church of England, it was natural that there should be Professors of Divinity and that they should be accorded a position of precedence. But now that all our universities justly pride themselves upon their freedom, and in particular are free from religious tests, theological faculties would seem to be an anomalous survival. The theologians themselves, though for obvious reasons they want theological faculties to continue, are by no means agreed about their *raison d'être*. A recent Regius Professor of Divinity at Oxford declared that the purpose of a theological faculty is to train ministers of religion, whereas the present Regius Professor at Cambridge has expressed the hope that the faculty of divinity there will never consent to be treated as 'a seminary for ordinands'.[2]

There is this to be said for the Oxford view, that nearly all students of theology in universities are candidates for ordination or intending specialists in the teaching of divinity in

[1] Reprinted with permission, from *Encounter*, September 1956.
[2] See J. Burnaby, *Education, Religion, Learning and Research* (1953), p. 18.

schools, just as nearly all university teachers of theology are ministers of one or other of the churches and so are professionally committed to maintaining the truth of Christianity. But why should Christianity be privileged in free universities, and why should the training of Christian propagandists benefit from the largesse with which the State sustains university education? Why should not the upholders of other philosophies of life—humanists, positivists, and communists, for example— also have fair shares? It is not easy to see the answer to these questions.

If, on the other hand, it is claimed, as at Cambridge, that the function of theological teachers is not to maintain the truth of Christianity, but to convey a knowledge of its history, and that this can be done with the same objectivity and freedom from bias as are required in all other academic teachers, then different, but no less awkward, questions arise. In genuinely free and non-confessional universities where neither teachers nor students are tied to any one set of beliefs, should not Christianity be studied purely as an historical phenomenon and in relation to other religions and cultures, i.e. as part of the comparative study of religions? Then most of what is at present called theology or divinity could be treated as what it really is, namely, a department of historical studies. What could not thus be subsumed under the study of history could be taken over by other faculties. The teaching of Hebrew and Greek and Latin could be supplied by the appropriate language faculties, and in so far as theology embarks upon a constructive or systematic, as distinguished from a purely historical, study of ethical and religious ideas, the philosophers should be able to provide what is needed. On these grounds and on grounds of economy a good case could be made out for the liquidation of theological faculties as separate institutions.

However, no one in or out of theological faculties seems at

present to be contemplating this possibility. So far from existing faculties being threatened with dissolution into their com-
ponent parts, new ones are being founded and built up in
modern universities. It is all very incongruous and puzzling,
like the illogical ways of other English institutions to which we
are accustomed. Happily, although theological faculties in
universities are the most obvious centres of theological activity
in England and are presumably the nurseries of future theologians, the future of theology can be considered without regard
to the academic puzzles which we have so far been noticing
and which have left us in the dark about what, if anything,
makes theology a distinct intellectual discipline and field of
investigation.

Definitions may be the refuge of third-rate minds, but they
can be useful in helping us to ascertain what we are supposed
to be talking about. The dictionary indicates clearly enough
what biology is, and zoology, and geology, and anthropology.
What then does it say theology is? 'The study or science which
treats of God, His nature and attributes, and His relations with
man and the universe' (O.E.D.). It sounds a pretty tall and all-
embracing order. I can introduce, right away, one limiting
factor. The O.E.D. definition, as it stands, might be taken to
apply to Mohammedan or Hindu, as well as to Christian,
theology. I have no competence to write about the past, let
alone the future, of Mohammedan or Hindu theology; I can
deal only with Christian theology, i.e. theology as it has been
understood and studied by Christians.

The most striking thing about Christian theology, or rather
Christian theologians, is their confidence—which is in the
nature of a presupposition—that the *Theos* or God, from whom
theology derives its name, has revealed himself or made himself known to human beings, and indeed that he does so still.
It is held that he reveals himself not only in the passive sense

in which a sunset may be said to reveal itself to a poet or an artist, but actively by taking the initiative. Theology presupposes that God is Person or Subject and acts as such, and that he is not merely a thing or an object. It follows that, if theologians are to be faithful to this presupposition of their study, they will not be content with the methods of abstraction, analysis and classification employed by other sciences. 'The business of academic man', Dr Austin Farrer has said, 'is to master his subject-matter, and religion presents a subject-matter which, by her own admission, can never be mastered.'[1] We miss much of the truth, perhaps the most important truth, about a human person if we regard him as a thing or an object and do no more than study in abstraction from one another the various elements in his make-up, if we break him up or break him down, so to speak, or if we treat him as just one of a class. By these methods we may get to know a lot *about* him, without ever getting to know him as a unique individual and without ever taking in what he has to say to us. *A fortiori* that must apply to God as he is conceived by theology. It may be incredible that God is personal and knowable as persons are knowable, but the presupposition that he is so is what makes theology a distinct study or science, and it is also what gives theology an interest different from that of history or philosophy or ethics. Only if this essential presupposition of theology is taken seriously, can it have a contemporary importance and a future worthy of consideration.

But there is a further point that must be made about this essential presupposition of theology. The presupposition is not only that there is a Supreme Being who is capable of making himself known to mankind, but that in fact he has done so, above all through his dealings with a particular people (the

[1] Article on 'The Queen of Sciences' in *The Twentieth Century*, June 1955, p. 491.

Hebrews) and in a particular course of events which culminated in the 'advent' or coming of Jesus Christ. This again may
be incredible, and is certainly scandalous to all who suppose
that, if there were a God who could reveal himself, he ought
to have done so universally and simultaneously to the whole
human race. The offensive character of the belief that God has
limited and entrusted a revelation, that should be for all men,
to a 'peculiar' people (the Hebrews before Christ, the Christians
after Christ) is frankly acknowledged by perceptive theologians: they call it 'the scandal of particularity'. But it is this
belief—this presupposed belief—that distinguishes theology
from the general history of religions and from metaphysics: it
is this that gives it its distinct or peculiar interest.

Theology then is the study or science which consists in
investigating all that is involved in the essential theological presupposition. While it includes assertions about history which
must be examined by the most rigorous methods of historical
criticism, it includes much else besides. We cannot here survey
the development of theology from the Bible onwards, but in
order to take the measure of the crisis in which theology is at
present involved, and upon the resolution of which its future
will depend, it is necessary to take into account what has
happened during the last two centuries.

Two hundred years ago and even more recently, nearly all
theologians, as well as the whole body of Christians, took it
for granted not only that a Divine Revelation had been given,
but also that it was finally fixed in an inerrant book, the Holy
Bible. In words spoken by a Professor of Divinity at Durham
in 1834: 'There is nothing to discover in Revelation. The
province of the human understanding with respect to scripture is to believe and to obey it.'[1] Catholic and Protestant

[1] H. J. Rose, quoted by A. M. Ramsey, *Jesus Christ in Faith and History*
(1940), p. 2.

theologians shared this assumption: their differences concerned the question where the divinely appointed authority for interpreting the Bible was to be found—in tradition, the creeds, the consensus of the Fathers of the Church, the pronouncements of General Councils, the decisions of the popes, or the testimony of the individual conscience informed by the Holy Spirit. There was plenty here to argue about and to provide matter for sectarian disputations. The point is that all shared the assumption, which they looked upon as absolutely firm standing-ground, that the Bible was a holy island in the ocean of secular literature, exempt from the scrutiny of profane minds. What has happened during the last two centuries is that this assumption, with which the essential theological presupposition had come to be identified, has been made untenable. It has been undermined.

The undermining process was a complex one, as in the case of other traditional beliefs. I will mention three of the things that shattered the basis of what may conveniently be called 'traditional orthodoxy'. First, the literary and historical criticism of the Bible, and its comparison with other ancient literatures, destroyed the notion that, it is a holy island in the ocean of secular literature, or that there is a sharp dichotomy between what is sacred and secular and between what is natural and supernatural. Secondly, well-established discoveries made through the natural and human sciences showed that the Bible contains many mistaken statements and that belief in its inerrancy is no longer tenable. Thirdly, the disintegration of traditional philosophy, whether scholastic or cartesian and its displacement by other philosophies—empirical, immanentist, positivist, etc.—resulted in there no longer being any common and congenial framework of ideas or universe of discourse within which the Bible could be interpreted and theological beliefs could be commended.

Theologians and their followers have reacted to these solvents in, roughly speaking, three ways. First, there have been those who have said *non possumus* to all that conflicted with traditional orthodoxy, and have determined to make no concessions to disturbing facts or to dangerous thoughts. At least, they have made only minor concessions and adjustments, and then with the utmost reluctance and at the latest possible date. Often this kind of reaction, usually called 'fundamentalist', is very crudely expressed, but sometimes it is maintained with much subtlety, as e.g. when Roman Catholic theologians defend their official doctrine of the inerrancy of the Bible.

Secondly, at the opposite extreme, there have been theologians who have not only acquiesced in the undermining of traditional orthodoxy, but have themselves played a leading part in the undermining operations. There have even been those who embraced modern discoveries and ideas with such enthusiasm and whole-heartedness that they have sacrificed the essential presupposition of theology in the process, i.e. the scandal of particularity. For example, a recent Nonconformist writer has remarked that 'with the passing of the old standardized, proof-text theology, the drift of Nonconformist liberalism was toward a vague humanism informed with Hegelian metaphysics and inspired with dreams of social progress'.[1] Or again, in a book on *The Kingdom of God in America* (by H. Richard Niebuhr) it was noted that 'a God without wrath brought men without sin into a kingdom without judgment through the ministrations of a Christ without a cross'. In other words, the suggestion is that these theologians, whom the 'fundamentalists' call 'modernists' or 'liberals' or worse names if they can think of them, in effect empty out the baby with the bath water.

Thirdly, between these two extremes, there has been a large

[1] G. O. Griffith, *The Theology of P. T. Forsyth*, (1948), p. 22.

variety of mediating theologians who have believed that they could adhere to, and vindicate, the essential theological presupposition, while interpreting the Bible by the ordinary canons of literary and historical criticism, accepting all well-established scientific discoveries, and being philosophically open-minded. These mediating theologians have probably been more in evidence in Britain than elsewhere: partly owing to our native genius for compromise and for steering middle courses, and also, in the case of Anglican theologians, owing to the circumstance that, however much they might be carried away by the radical theories of continental scholars when in their studies and their lecture rooms, they still had, when they went to church or chapel, to use and make sense of the Book of Common Prayer in which there is no getting away from the essential presupposition of theology.

Perhaps I ought to notice a fourth type of reaction to the undermining of traditional orthodoxy, namely the reaction to 'modernist' or 'liberal' theology which is sometimes called 'neo-orthodoxy' and is associated principally with the names of Professors Karl Barth and Emil Brunner. But this is only a special example of what I call a mediating theological position. The learned American ultra-conservative theologian, Dr Cornelius van Til,[1] has—quite rightly from his point of view—attacked Barth and Brunner as 'the New Modernists'!

The question about the future of theology can now be formulated thus: If theology has a future, is it likely to lie with the 'fundamentalists', with the 'modernists', with the mediating theologians, or with none of them? All theologians have their hopes about the answer to this question: no one can know the answer. I will content myself with a few comments on the possible answers. It must be borne in mind that, if theology is to

[1] See his book, *The New Modernism: an Appraisal of the Theology of Barth and Brunner* (1946).

have a future at all comparable with its past, it has an immense
amount of lost ground that it must recover; especially it will
have to re-engage the interest of educated laymen and to get
on to speaking terms with scientists, philosophers and all kinds
of men of action, most of whom are at present on or beyond
the frontiers of the churches.

The future of theology is unlikely to be in the hands of the
'fundamentalists' unless the flight to religion combined with
the flight from reason, of which Billy Graham's crusades are
symbolic, spreads much further than it has done yet. Even so,
it would not be an imposing or a protracted future, if there is
any foundation for the maxim, 'Magna est veritas, et prae-
valet.' It is a fact that Billy Graham not long ago conducted a
mission in the university church at Cambridge, and there is
nowadays a good deal of 'fundamentalist' religion in the
student world, not least among medical students. But we may
doubt whether much importance need be attached to what
may be only an undergraduate mood or fashion.

The future of theology is unlikely to rest with the 'modernists', not because their thinking is too radical or revolutionary, but because, as I have already suggested, they tend to
sacrifice the essential presupposition of theology on the inade-
quately criticized altar of 'modern thought'. If people in future
want theology at all, they are likely to want the real thing,
that is, a theology that can speak with conviction, and carry
conviction, about a God who has revealed himself as the Judge
and Deliverer of mankind, and upon whom the origin and
destiny of the race manifestly depend.

Does the future then lie with the mediating theologians?
This also seems unlikely. The ablest of them are to be found in
the universities and, as we have seen, they are there chiefly
employed in instructing candidates for the ministry and teachers
of divinity. Academic theologians may carry conviction

to their pupils and supply their needs. But few of them have so far shown a capacity for convincing laymen engaged in other disciplines and walks of life that theology has anything to say to them or to do with them. Yet theology, if its presupposition is valid, is a subject that must vitally concern everyone. No one in his senses will suppose that there is a God who has revealed himself only for the benefit of clergymen and teachers of divinity. Actually, our university faculties of theology, as at present constituted, would provide little or no scope for theologians qualified to show what their subject had to do with the problems and decisions that confront laymen in the public and private life of the work-a-day world. I do not know where theologians so qualified—for example, Reinhold Niebuhr or Paul Tillich in the U.S.A. or the late Dietrich Bonhoeffer in Germany or that remarkable woman Simone Weil—could be placed in an English university faculty of theology. Even if there were such places available, there are few, if any, English theologians who would be capable of occupying them.

If theology is to have a future of any consequence, we may hazard the conjecture that it will have to cease to be an almost clerical monopoly. It will have to win the interest of laymen. It will have to command their intellectual respect and to capture their imagination and then give them free scope to play their part in theological thinking, and by laymen I do not mean only men already in the pew. There have been notable lay theologians in the past, for instance, Dr Johnson and William Blake in the eighteenth century, and in the nineteenth century S. T. Coleridge, R. H. Hutton, Editor of *The Spectator*, and J. H. Shorthouse, the industrialist and novelist, not to mention some Victorian prime ministers.

My forecast is that, if there is a revival of theology, it will be primarily the work of laymen. There are in this connexion not yet many, but there are a few, signs of promise. I am told that laymen are taking more interest than clergymen in the writings of Rudolf Bultmann, which are now appearing in English. Bultmann, with his radical emphasis on the need to 'demythologize' the gospel and reinterpret it in terms that at once retain its essence and make it meaningful for men living in the twentieth century, is certainly on the target. Books by theologians that succeed in showing that theology has to do with the profoundest and most baffling of contemporary issues—e.g. Dietrich Bonhoeffer's *Letters and Papers from Prison*—ring bells for laymen who are quite untouched by conventional clerical theologizing. It is my own experience that there is more interest in the basic theological questions, as distinguished from what is secondary or trivial, among laymen outside as well as inside the churches than there is in many clerical circles. But there is no ground here for complacency about the future of theology, nor indeed for confidence unless there be truth in the seventeenth-century adage that man's extremity is God's opportunity.

III

FREEDOM AND RESPONSIBILITY[1]

THERE is a saying of G. K. Chesterton's that I am fond of quoting: 'If I wish to dissuade a man from drinking his tenth whisky and soda, I slap him on the back and say, "Be a man!" No one who wished to dissuade a crocodile from eating its tenth explorer would slap it on the back and say, "Be a crocodile!" '

The first question I want to consider about freedom and responsibility is summed up in that witticism. Crocodiles cannot help themselves; it is their nature to eat explorers whenever they get the chance of doing so. You must not blame them. They are not free to do otherwise. They are *determined* to eat explorers, not in the sense that they have considered the matter and determined amongst themselves that it is a good idea—not in the sense that they have passed a resolution that they will eat explorers; but in the sense that it is settled and determined for them, and they have no choice in the matter. And therefore they are not responsible for what they do; they are not to be blamed or praised for anything that they do, because they are not ever free to do otherwise.

It is popularly supposed that the case with human beings is different. It is popularly supposed that we are capable of determining for ourselves what we will do; that we are free to choose on rational grounds between one course of action and another; that we are responsible for what we do, and therefore that there is some sense in our being praised or blamed for

[1] A lecture delivered at Balls Park College, Hertford, on 9 May 1955.

40

what we do, as there would not be if we could not help ourselves or determine ourselves. Not only are these things popularly supposed, but they appear in practice to be taken for
granted in learned and academic assemblies. A. C. Benson[1]
tells us that Henry Sidgwick, the Cambridge philosopher,
used to say that he had in early life been very shy, but that
realizing that it was a social duty to talk, he had determined
always to talk, whether he had anything to say or not. And so
he had overcome his shyness, and he imagined that he had done
so by self-determination. Or let me speak for myself: I am
accustomed to blame myself. For instance, if I have played a
very bad round of golf (as all too often I do) I say to myself:
'This really won't do, Vidler. Next time you must play
better; you must keep your eye on the ball when you're
driving'—and I imagine that I am free to do that. Whereas if
I was a cow, there would be no point in my saying to myself:
'Now, Bluebell, that was a very poor yield of milk; you really
must give more tomorrow,'—because cows cannot help
themselves; they are not responsible.

Even in Chesterton's example of the man who is about to
take his tenth whisky and soda and so is probably in a position
no longer to exercise much control over himself, still he is
held responsible for having allowed himself to get into that
condition.

The first question before us is whether this supposed freedom
and responsibility of human beings is a fact or an illusion. It
is not only intellectually sophisticated people who sometimes
argue that it is an illusion. Years ago there was a Lancashire
artisan who said, 'No man is responsible for his character or
actions. Iron is hard, and lead is soft. But you don't praise iron
for its hardness or blame lead for its softness. So one man is
born naturally brave and another naturally timid. But there's

[1] *Leaves of the Tree* (1911), p. 55.

41

no sense in praising one or blaming the other. I blame no one.'
'I blame no one.' That is obviously the only rational attitude,
if human freedom and responsibility are illusory. What then
is the truth of the matter?

Before we go any further, we might spend a moment or two
in defining our principal terms. A great many discussions and
arguments are bedevilled through a failure to define the terms
that are being used. In the present instance, I have taken the
trouble to look up the words 'free' and 'responsible' in the
Oxford English Dictionary. I found that the adjective 'free' has
thirty-two different meanings, so it could obviously be a fertile
source of confusion. However, the meaning we are concerned
with, at any rate at this stage, is, I take it, as follows: 'of a
person, his will, etc. Acting of one's own will or choice, and
not under compulsion or constraint; determining one's own
action or choice, not motived from without.' To put it more
simply, Bishop Berkeley, the famous philosopher, said: 'A
man is said to be free, so far forth as he can do what he will.'

'Responsible' is a word that is less used and has fewer meanings. The *Oxford English Dictionary* lists only six. Ours is as
follows: 'Morally accountable for one's actions; capable of
rational conduct.' The ideas of responsibility and freedom are
closely connected as appears from this definition of Sir Walter
Moberly's: 'A man is morally responsible for his actions in
proportion as he is their originating cause.'[1]

I propose now to call attention to some of the arguments
that can be adduced in favour of the view that man is not free
and responsible; in other words, arguments for what is called
'determinism' or what used to be called 'necessitarianism'.
The case for determinism can be stated on various grounds,
though their general effect is the same.

For example, it can be maintained that your character was

[1] *Responsibility*. Riddell Memorial Lectures (1951), p. 5.

settled in advance by the chromosomes that you happen to inherit from your parents. You may think you are the architect of your own character, but really it was fixed before you were born. That is the biological form of the argument. Or again, on the ground of psychology it can be held that the motives of our actions are not what we consciously imagine them to be but have their real springs in the unconscious—which is to say that we are not responsible for them. For instance, I hold very strongly that in a cup of tea the milk should always be poured in after the tea, and I could give you at least twenty reasons for that; but if I was psycho-analysed, it might appear that my strong feelings on this subject have nothing to do with my supposed reasons, but are due to the fact that in my childhood I had an awful contretemps with an aunt who happened to take her tea the other way . . . so awful a contretemps that it has ever since been buried in my unconscious.

A third form of the argument for determinism is economic or social. People imagine that they act, or vote, on disinterested rational grounds. They imagine that they have freely and responsibly come to the conclusion that such and such a policy will make for the national well-being;—but what in fact determines their acts or their votes is their private or class interest. Why is it, for instance, that when I lived in the slums of Newcastle-on-Tyne my neighbours mostly voted Labour, whereas in Windsor my neighbours mostly vote Conservative? It is not to be supposed that they have each individually thought out their political creed and by a strange coincidence have come to the same conclusion. Evidently their opinions in either case are the result of their membership of a particular social class.

On these and similar grounds, a theory can be worked out that our freedom and responsibility are illusory. If we were in possession of all the facts about ourselves, we should see that everything we think or do or say is the result of biological, psychological or economic causation. We imagine that we are rational beings but really we are creatures of instinct. So pervasive is this illusion that we are rational and morally responsible beings, that we go so far as to attribute the same sort of freedom to our domestic animals. We see a dog hesitate between the alternatives of chasing sheep and obeying his master; we fancy there is a moral struggle going on in the dog, and if he does what we think is right we call him a good dog. But all that has really happened is that there has been a conflict between two desires or instinctive tendencies; the tendency to chase sheep and the tendency to fear the punishment which past experience has shown to follow such behaviour. When it is pointed out, we can see that we deceive ourselves in attributing moral responsibility to animals. We are not prepared to make the same acknowledgment about ourselves because it would be too humiliating. But if we were candid should we not have to say of ourselves, 'How free we seem, how fettered fast we lie'? The case for determinism is in fact stronger than most unsophisticated people suppose.

What is there to be said on the other side? Some people think that determinism can be refuted by a very simple argument. If determinism is true, it must follow that some people are determined to think it is true and other people to think it is not true; but nobody is free to form a rational opinion on the subject, and so neither opinion can be more reasonable than the other. That is not a proof that determinism is false. What it does show however is that, if determinism is true, no one can ever prove that it is true because none of us is free to think otherwise than we do think.

That is an important point, a logical point; but there are more important things to be considered. As a matter of fact, whatever theory we hold, is it not the case that we all *act* on the assumption that we are free and responsible? The fact that we go on discussing the question of determinism, the fact that the determinist thinks it worth while going on trying to convince those who do not agree with him, is evidence that he himself in practice believes that men are free to form rational and responsible opinions—else he would be merely wasting his breath.

Again, in practice we all praise or blame other people from time to time. If on a Sunday morning the paper boy leaves at your house the *News of the World* instead of the *Observer* or vice versa—you do not say, 'Of course he couldn't help it': you blame him. You can be sure that the Lancashire artisan who said, 'I blame no one', was not in practice beyond blaming his children if they caused him displeasure or his political opponents for what he considered to be the error in their opinions. Likewise, those of us who in a philosophical argument may maintain the determinist position have no scruple in the affairs of daily life in praising or blaming people—which means that in practice we accept the assumption that men are free and responsible. This does not of course finally settle the matter, because the universal practice of mankind might be founded on a universal illusion. At the same time, if we really thought or seriously suspected that that was the case, we had best pack up and give up discussing this or anything else, since there would be no reason to suppose that we could arrive at the truth about anything. We do continue to study and discuss these questions; it is reasonable to suspect that there must be a fallacy in a theory upon which no one does or can act consistently.

I should myself say that deterministic arguments or theories direct our attention to important ranges of truth. They break down only when they are presented as the *whole* truth. It is a fundamental datum of our personal experience that in the living moment of decision we are free and responsible, and it is very difficult to see how the idea that we are so could ever have arisen in our minds if it were not a fact.[1] It has never occurred to a tiger or to a chaffinch that he is free and responsible; if it did occur to him, then he would be free and responsible. If a theory—in this case, complete determinism—contradicts a fundamental datum of human experience, so much the worse for the theory.

But we can understand how this particular contradiction or misunderstanding arises, and how it is that intelligent people have entertained a theory by which, if it were true, they would be completely stultified. I said that it is in the living moment of decision that we know ourselves to be free—which is to say, not completely determined. But the living moments of decision are all the time passing into the dead past, which *is* completely determined. At the present moment, I am free to decide between blowing my nose and not blowing my nose: the present and the future are in that respect undetermined or indeterminate, and I can myself determine them. But what happened five minutes ago or even five seconds ago is determined and cannot be altered, however free and responsible I am in the present and however free and responsible I was then.

In the living moment of decision, I am, as it were, a participant in the game of life; when I theorize about it as a scientist or a philosopher, I stand back from it and look upon it as a spectator, from whose point of view it is all determined. When the various sciences, such as biology or psychology or economics, study human life and form theories about it, they—rightly and inevitably—study it as it exists in the dead past or at least as it exists outside themselves, where it *is* determined and fixed.

[1] Cp. J. Oman, *Grace and Personality*[2] (1919), p. 41.

Only in that way is it possible for it to be studied by scientific methods.

Each science aims at arranging and coordinating the phenomena with which it is concerned into an orderly system. It works with the concept of causation, and seeks to show how its facts are knit together in a chain of cause and effect. The dead past can be studied as a fixed, impersonal chain of cause and effect, and very useful results are reached in this way. In this way too you can make practical calculations about what is likely to happen in the future. But there is no logical or other necessity that what you predict will actually come to pass, for in the future, as distinguished from the past, there is the incalculable factor of human freedom and responsibility—not to mention divine freedom. As Lord Oxford and Asquith said, 'Personality is still the most potent factor in the world, and as long as some men die at forty-five and others live to be ninety, political prophecy will be a fond and futile art.'[1] Other forms of prophecy aren't futile, but none of them is infallible. You can generally prophesy what a machine will do, but you will not invariably be right. It is said that once upon a time the preacher in College Chapel at Eton on a Sunday morning was dealing with the subject of infallibility and during his sermon the school clock began to strike: 'There now', declared the preacher, 'I can show you what infallibility means: you know infallibly that the clock will strike twelve times.' But the clock rose to the occasion and proceeded to strike 132 times!

Only what is past is infallibly determined. But because the past cannot be altered once it has happened, it does not follow that there was a cast-iron necessity governing it before it happened. It is a confusion between those two things that prevents people from seeing that there is no real contradiction between

[1] See Spender and Asquith, *Life of Lord Oxford and Asquith* (1932), i. 66.

the truth in theories of determinism and the fact of human freedom and responsibility.

I conclude then, so far, that we really are free and responsible. At the same time, I should wish to urge that we ought to acknowledge the truth in deterministic theories. Our freedom and responsibility are exercised within very definite limits, and there are powerful influences playing upon us all the time which we may fail to perceive. We are far from being so purely and simply free as we are inclined to imagine. Our biological inheritance, our psychological make-up, and our economic status, as well as the context of events in which we have to act, all set limits within which we have to exercise our freedom and responsibility. Freud and Marx and the rest can help us a great deal to understand the conditions of our life and the influences that are playing upon us. An understanding of these things will enable us to act more freely and responsibly than we should otherwise be able to do. If, for example, I understand how powerfully my economic interests can influence my political judgment, then I shall be able to be on my guard against allowing them to be so unduly. What we are responsible for is not the conditions, favourable or unfavourable, with which we start life, or which come our way, but the use we make of them and the way we deal with them.

Those are the principal things I want to say about the general subject of freedom and responsibility, and that ends the first part—the philosophical part—of this essay. I now turn to part two in which I am going to consider the Christian attitude, or what theology has to say about these things.

And, first, the Christian attitude to what we have been considering so far. The Bible does not contain any formal arguments to show that man is free and responsible, nor does it contain a formal refutation of complete determinism. No church expects us to recite a creed in which we formally state:

I believe that human beings are free and responsible. On the other hand, there can be no doubt that the Bible and the Church everywhere take it for granted that men are free and responsible in the sense we have been discussing; and the whole Christian scheme of things presupposes that that is so.

One might almost say that the Bible's definition of man is that he is a being who can freely respond to God and who is answerable to God. I have maintained elsewhere[1] that the sense of responsibility or moral accountability we all have in greater or less degree—the sense that there are some things we ought never to do whatever the social or other pressure put upon us—can be satisfactorily explained only if we are really responsible for what we do to *God*, and not merely to ourselves or to society,—in other words, if in the final analysis duty is owed not merely to the State or to ourselves but to a Transcendent Being who is above all States and all individuals and entitled to the obedience of them all.

Actually however, what the Bible and Christianity have chiefly to say about freedom and responsibility begins more or less where we have so far left off. While the Bible takes for granted that we are free in the rudimentary sense of being able (within definite limits) to do what we want, and that we are answerable to God for what we do and do not do, yet it is more concerned to say that in a deeper sense we are in bondage and need to be made free. In a sense different from that intended by Rousseau, we may say that according to the Bible 'man is born free, but is everywhere in chains'.

'Everywhere in chains.' This brings us to the question of what is meant by 'original sin'. 'Original sin' is not happily so-called. The fact it is intended to point to is not the original or primary fact about man, nor is it sin in the same sense as sins for which we are plainly and obviously responsible like telling

[1] See my *Christian Belief* (1950), Chapter I.

lies or losing our tempers.[1] At the same time, it ought not to be too difficult for us to see—the state of the world being what it is—that the human race is in bondage to some hostile force or has some tragic disease at its heart. Why is it that man seems 'strangely balanced between an unquenchable impulse to build and an implacable impulse to destroy'? Why is it that man who 'has been given a rich, fertile and productive world' sets himself to turn it into a desert? 'Why is it that man, endued with every gift needed to master the world, is so wholly incapable of ruling himself? Why is it that man, made to love and to be loved should expend so much of his energy in useless hate?'[2]

The doctrine of 'original sin' is designed to account for this strange contradiction, this tragic surd, that there is in our human existence—which comes out in all periods of history, and in all parts of the world, in one way or another; it is in fact universal. It seems to be an inescapable part of our lot, and yet—and this is why it is appropriately called 'sin'—we feel answerable for it—we do not just sit down under it and accept it as our necessary fate; we know human life ought not to be as it is and need not be as it is; we are all involved in responsibility for the fact that it is so.

But this 'original sin' is not just a general characteristic of the race; it is not something that is true only of societies and civilizations. It is a thing of which we can each be aware in our individual selves whether or no we call it 'original sin'. I know that I am made to live in dependence on God and in harmony with my fellows; and that I am not meant to make myself the centre of the world. But I seem to be cursed with an inevitable tendency to treat myself as the centre of the

---

[1] 'We are bound to say that only where individual knowledge and responsibility begin does personal guilt begin.'—C. Gore, *The Holy Spirit and the Church* (1924), p. 329.

[2] See Stephen Neill, *Christian Faith Today* (1955), Chapter 5.

world, to look at everything from my own point of view, to ask myself, first, how this or that will affect me, to excuse myself and to blame other people. Quite apart from or prior to my particular actual sins, I seem to be inevitably egocentric—self-excusing, self-justifying: inevitably, and yet I am ashamed of being so, I feel guilty for my self-centredness however inevitable it may be. I am in bondage to a self that is not my real self, that is not the self that God meant and means me to be.

If what I have just said rings any sort of bell in your own experience, then you will know for yourself what is meant by 'original sin', and you will see the force of the statement that, if in one sense we are free, in another and profounder sense we are in bondage. We are in bondage to that little demon—the ego within each of us. 'It is from my likings that I must be emancipated if I would be a freeman,' said Frederick Denison Maurice.[1] We are in bondage to all the conflicting impulses and instincts which push and pull us in different directions and run away with us before we realize what has happened . . . pride and jealousy, ambition and sloth, covetousness and discontent. And the irony of the situation is that the more we try to release ourselves from this bondage the more we get ourselves into further bondage, like the fly who tries to escape from the spider's web.

That comes out in what the Bible says about the law of God. According to the Old Testament the law of God was given by God to his people after their deliverance from bondage to Egypt to enable them to live wholesomely and harmoniously, as God wanted them to live. But the Jews took hold of the law of God, which was meant to set them free, and turned it into a new kind of bondage which we call legalism. They so elaborated the law of God that by the time Christ came it

[1] *The Conscience*[2] (1872), p. 117.

had become a collection of finicky rules and regulations by which the best of them, that is the Pharisees, were completely tied and bound. It is all too easy to become slaves of a system, even of a highly moral system.

When Christ came, he came to set men free from this bondage to the law in which the best of men had got themselves bogged down. The law, as St Paul said, was in itself holy and good; nevertheless he could praise God that through Christ he had been delivered from bondage to the law and that Christ was the end of the law to everyone that believes. What he meant was that in Christ God had met mankind at the point of its final predicament. If by our own most moral efforts we cannot set ourselves free, our only hope is that God will come and set us free—by giving us a new centre from which to live and a new spirit in which we may do his will spontaneously. Then we shall no longer be rooted and centred in ourselves, but can be rooted and built up in him. The Christian experience is that God has thus set men free, and that all who will put their trust in Christ, in whose service is perfect freedom, are liberated from the final human predicament and can have a real foretaste, even in this world, of what true freedom is, 'the glorious liberty of the children of God'.

In the New Testament this experience of living in a new freedom in Christ and in the power of his Spirit is described or expressed in various ways, for instance in the idea of being justified by grace through faith apart from works (the works of the law),—or in the idea of eternal life being freely given to men here and now as a present reality,—or in our being able already to 'taste the powers of the age to come'.

It might be a good thing if we called the former rudimentary freedom *free-will*, to distinguish it from this higher kind of freedom which is the glorious liberty of the children of God. *Free-will* then is what I was speaking about in the first half of this essay: it means merely ability to choose between two alternatives, to choose what is good or what is bad. But *freedom* —Christian freedom—means being set free to choose spontaneously and without strain or conflict always what is best. The grace of God does not compel us to choose what is best, but it enables us to do so freely of our own accord.

This brings me to the last of the big questions connected with freedom and responsibility that I want to touch upon. I mean the question of predestination. At first sight it might seem that Christianity delivers us from the devil of complete determinism only to desposit us in the deep sea of divine predestination. What point is there in being declared free from bondage to our passions and instincts, to chromosomes and economic interests, if instead it is to be declared that our destiny was fixed in advance by an immutable decree of God and there is nothing we can do to alter it? If we really value freedom and responsibility, is there any reason why we should prefer the higher slavery to the power? Vast tomes have been written on this subject. Only a few points can be made here.

First, although the word 'predestination' does not occur in the Bible, there is no doubt that a belief which that term fairly suggests does run through the Bible and is even more in evidence in the New Testament than in the Old. I have met people who imagine they can dismiss the whole idea of predestination as a fantastic aberration of Calvinism. Such people cannot be very well acquainted with their Bibles, and usually they know very little about Calvinism either.

Secondly, I should admit that there are doctrines of predestination, of which that associated with Calvinism, is one, that are morally intolerable. The notion that God arbitrarily decided before our births that some of us should go to the bliss of heaven and others to everlasting torment in hell is to represent God as being so repulsive in character as to make nonsense of the Christian faith. Indeed, the fact that many presumably good and intelligent people do appear to have entertained this notion of predestination, and to have done so with equanimity, should make us suspect that there is more in the whole idea than meets the eye. And there is, indeed there is. It is true, on the one hand, that predestination stands for something that is quite fundamental in the Christian faith, but, on the other hand, in some of the forms in which it has been worked out into a theological system it has been turned into a travesty of Christianity.

So thirdly, I ask what is the fundamental point in the idea of divine predestination? It is this. All Christians who know their stuff will tell you that man's salvation, his liberation and new life in Christ, originate in the will of God and not in the will of man. This is expressed clearly in Christ's words to his disciples, 'Ye have not chosen me but I have chosen you.' That is gospel truth about all Christians and not only about the first disciples. Is not this gospel, good news—namely that your final destiny, your hope of eternal life, depends upon, and is founded in, the will of God and not your own will? For the will of God is firm, reliable, trustworthy; whereas our own wills, as we know too well, are fickle, unreliable, untrustworthy. The doctrine of predestination is an attempt to put this fundamental Christian conviction into the form of a theological proposition. The proposition is that those who are being saved are foreordained to salvation. The logical corollary of this, that those who will not be saved in the end are foreordained to perdition, is not drawn in the New Testament or at any rate is not emphasized. And that is a sign that what the New Testament is concerned to assert is the positive truth that the setting free of mankind from every kind of bondage originates in the will of God and is carried through by the will of God; in other words, that it is for us gratefully to accept and respond to the free life in Christ which God has prepared for us. The originating cause of a man's salvation is in the grace of God, the goodwill of God, towards him, and not in his own choice.

Fourthly, if that is the positive and the wholesome truth in the idea of predestination, it provides no warrant for the systematic and logical negative conclusions that have been drawn from it, especially perhaps in Calvinism. While we ought not to despise logic, certainly not when it means thinking clearly about our experience, yet when it runs away on abstract and speculative conclusions which bear no relation to experience we have every reason to distrust it. The God of Christian experience is not a God who arbitrarily consigns people to heaven or hell for no intelligible reason whatever. The doctrine of predestination, properly understood, means not that God has arbitrarily foreordained some people to heaven and others to hell, but that every man and all men are foreordained to eternal life in so far as they are in Christ and accept from Christ the freedom wherewith he has made men free, and that every man and all men are foreordained to eternal loss or eternal death in so far as they refuse the offer of life and freedom in Christ and determine to make themselves the centre of the world. I do not think this is an attempt to evade a difficulty in the Bible; on the contrary, that is the whole tenor of the Bible's message.

But fifthly and finally, there is no doubt an outstanding difficulty or paradox. At one point in Christopher Fry's play *The Dark is Light Enough* the heroine says something like this: 'There's one moment, the decisive moment, when the will is not free.' It seems to me that the profoundest Christians have firmly grasped this nettle and have confessed that not only were they not masters of their fate, but that they had not even got sufficient virtue in them freely to accept what was gratuitously offered them in Christ. They had to be enslaved by

Christ in order to be truly liberated. That is to say, at the decisive moment, at the decisive turning point in Christian experience, we are not free but are blessedly enslaved.

C. S. Lewis in his autobiography has a chapter about his conversion which is entitled 'Checkmate'. In the course of this he writes:

> Before God closed in on me, I was in fact offered what now appears a moment of wholly free decision. . . . The choice appeared to be momentous but it was also strangely unemotional. I was moved by no desires or fears. In a sense I was not moved by anything. I chose to open, to unbuckle, to loosen the rein. I say 'I chose', yet it did not really seem possible to do the opposite. . . . Necessity may not be the opposite of freedom, and perhaps a man is most free when, instead of producing motives, he could only say, 'I am what I do'.[1]

But when a man is thus taken captive by Christ, he is not held in captivity; Christ takes men captive in order to make them really free. That is the last Christian word about freedom. This is the freedom that is created not by Law but by Love. This is the freedom of which St Augustine said: 'Love, and do what you will.' This is the freedom of which we can experience only a foretaste or an earnest in this world, but it is enough to convince us that at last it is the only freedom worth having.

[1] C. S. Lewis, *Surprised by Joy* (1955), pp. 211f.

56

IV

HISTORY ACCORDING TO
THE BIBLE[1]

I

IT is disconcerting, when you have accepted an invitation
to speak about 'History according to the Bible', to find
that the Bible does not appear to say anything about
'history'. The word 'history' does not occur, so far as I
have been able to discover, in any English version of the
Bible. Nor is this a purely verbal gap; it is not the case that
the Bible uses some other word or words for what we call
'history'; not only the word 'history' but the idea 'history' is
missing from the Bible.

But that is perhaps too sweeping. The Bible does contain
synonyms for some senses of the word 'history'. If by history
you mean a story, a particular narrative, chronicle or record of
events, the Bible does contain words for that. For instance,
Esther 6.1: 'On that night the king could not sleep; and he
gave orders to bring the book of memorable deeds, the
chronicles, and they were read before the king.' But we are
not concerned here with history in the sense of mere annals or
chronicles. We are concerned not with what you might find in
the Public Record Office or in the Royal Archives—not with
a heaping together of scenes and acts of which all that can be
said is that they happened—but with history as the complete
drama of human existence, if indeed it is a drama, which
presumably is one of the things that we want to know. And we
are concerned with history not in the sense of written accounts
of what has happened or written interpretations of the drama,
not with historiography or with methods of *writing* history—

[1] Two lectures given at the Student Christian Movement Study Conference at Swanwick in July 1949.

but with what has actually happened and does happen, with the drama itself—the stuff that forms the material of written history. What are we to make of that? Or rather, what does the Bible make of that?

Although the Bible doesn't use the word 'history', it contains plenty of historical material; it is full of such material. Nevertheless, it is worth remarking that, although the Bible is practically throughout dealing with history, it never says so; it never finds it necessary to use the category 'history' or to theorize about its subject. The Book of Genesis does not begin with an introductory essay or preface on the idea of history, but it charges straight in with 'In the beginning God created . . .'. This may be on my part no more than a rather laborious way of making the initial point that you will not find in the Bible 'a philosophy of history'. You will not find any systematic explanation of what history is. The Bible leaves it to philosophers to produce and to discuss philosophies of history; it supplies material for, but it betrays no direct interest in, that kind of inquiry.

But before we see what the Bible does do, it will be well to say a little more about what *we* mean by history, since we have got to use this word even if the Bible doesn't. The student of history is not entering a world of animal nature but a world which mankind has previously conquered by action, discovery, sacrifice and emotion. Here is one definition of history—a solemnly Teutonic one, which may serve our purpose: 'History is the totality of remembered events, which are determined by free human activity, and are important for the life of human groups' (Tillich). Consider the different elements in that definition. History is the *totality* of remembered events. That is to say, a single remembered event or a selection of remembered events could not constitute history; if we speak about 'history' like that, then we are concerned with the whole show—not just with one scene or one act. But it is *remembered* events with which we are concerned,—'memorable' might be an apter term. A vast number of things have happened and go on happening all the time which do not signify sufficiently for anyone to remember them, unless it be God, and I should be sorry to think that he has to remember every single thing that ever happens! It is very unlikely that you remember what you were doing at 2.15 p.m. on 10 January last, unless of course you keep a meticulously full diary; all the events that occur but are not remembered might be described as prehistoric— they are the stuff of which history is made, any of them might become historical and might have been woven into the pattern, but unless they are caught by the mesh of human memory they do not in fact become historical. Next, observe that historical events are determined by *free human activity*. That is to say, the sphere of history is to be distinguished, though it cannot be separated, from the sphere of nature. By 'nature' I mean here the natural environment—physical, biological, geographical, etc.—in which man lives, and which does not depend for its existence on free human activity; it would be there and go on even if man did not exist. Nature in this sense of course enters into history and shares in the shaping of history; but, except for a thoroughgoing naturalist, history is distinguished from nature as the sphere in which free human activity operates. Lastly, history consists of events that *are important for the life of human groups*. In other words, history is not biography though it may embrace biographies in so far as they are important for the life of a group. 'History is interested in the individual only as he has significance in a context of events wider than the individual.'[1] Events become historical only when they have a public meaning for some society, and when they acquire significance in a social tradition. 'Wherever a

[1] H. H. Farmer, *The World and God* (1935), p. 284.

social tradition exists', it has been said, 'however small and unimportant may be the society which is its vehicle, the possibility of history exists'.[1] So the action of an individual becomes historical only through his relation to a social group; this relation may take the form of *separation* from a society, as in the case of a hermit, but a hermit would be of no historical interest were he not related, at least negatively, to a society.

The Bible, though it does not contain the word 'history' and does not contain a philosophy of history even under another name, still says a great deal about 'the totality of remembered events, which are determined by free human activity and are important for the life of human groups'. The Bible, as we shall see, purports to deal with the whole of human history, and not only with a section of it. No doubt the Bible sees the history of mankind on a much smaller space-time scale than we do now; to us the Biblical history of the world is like a miniature of world-history. We are accustomed to paint it now on a much larger canvas, and to see it against a vaster space-time background. In the Bible the history of mankind is reduced to the scale of a few thousand years; but this is not to say that the meaning which the Bible sees in history may not be as significant and as true as it would be if it was seen on a larger scale. The meaning of a word or the truth of a description is not altered if you write it in larger or in smaller letters.

The way the Bible deals with history is to give a realistic description of it, to paint it, to portray it, using mythology and poetry as well as prose narratives for the purpose. It speaks to the imagination rather than to the discursive intellect. It contains no abstract disquisitions about the idea of history, and no theories about the course of civilization. It is not a study of history in the Toynbean sense. It is at no pains to assemble fine-sounding generalizations. You will find in the

[1] Christopher Dawson in *The Kingdom of God and History* (1938), p. 200.

Bible none of what Lord Acton called 'the slovenly use of the big brush'. So it does not discuss the philosophical difficulties that arise in all historical theories. The Bible does not take the trouble to see that all the things it says about history are consistent with one another; it leaves theologians to do that, and their efforts are not very impressive. The Bible does not claim that men, not even prophetic men, can get a complete understanding of history. It leaves much obscure. 'God makes visible to men his will in events, an obscure text, written in a mysterious language' (Victor Hugo). While the Bible holds that God has revealed to men as much as it is necessary for them to know, it says that there is much that God has not revealed and which men cannot know.

Commenting on Deut. 29.29, 'The secret things belong unto the Lord our God: but the things that are revealed belong unto us and to our children for ever, that we may do all the words of this law', Matthew Henry well says: 'Though God has kept much of his counsel secret, yet there is enough revealed to satisfy and save us. . . . All our knowledge must be in order to practise, for this is the end of all divine revelation, not to furnish us with curious subjects of speculation and discourse, which to entertain ourselves and our friends, *but that we may do all the words of this law*, and be blessed in the deed.'

What the Bible says about history has this limited and practical aim—to help its readers to see what are the real issues at stake in history; the great causes that are being advanced or thwarted by what men do or do not do; how they ought to act in history; not to answer all the questions about it that may occur to them. There is no unpragmatic speculating in the Bible.

One more introductory point to be noticed is that while the Bible deals with the universal history of mankind yet it does not pay equal attention to all periods and races but is selective in what it attends to. Not only does it attend chiefly to the history of one nation, but in the history of that one nation it attends chiefly to certain outstanding moments or crises. But in this it is true to the given character of history, or of biography for that matter. What the life of mankind or of a man is all about becomes manifest chiefly, perhaps only, at periodic moments of crisis; in the intervals between, its meaning lies more or less dormant and is hardly discernible. History can go to sleep and suddenly wake up. Henry Scott Holland once wrote to a friend: 'Perhaps it might help to remember that life is always a long pause in which we are preparing for some crisis or other: and these pause-times only get a meaning from the crisis when it comes. In themselves, they look meaningless and useless: but when the crisis or change arrives, we can judge of the pause, whether it was put to profit, or no.'[1] Those words are applicable to the history of nations as well as to the life of individuals; and they may explain why the Bible interprets the history of Israel in the light of a number of crises—the call of Abraham, the Exodus, the inthronization of David, the Exile and the Advent of Messiah—and has comparatively little to say about intervening periods. It follows from this that if we want to get at what the Bible says about history as a whole, we shall need to look especially at what it says about these great crises—the meaning which it sees in them, and which gives meaning to the long pause-times when nothing particularly meaningful seems to happen.

Even in what it says about the conditions that permanently govern historical existence, the Bible gives us not a set of abstract propositions nor a series of Gifford Lectures about the nature and destiny of man, but a mythology which takes the form of a description of critical moments in an imagined primitive history of mankind—the creation and fall, Babel and the

[1] See *Henry Scott Holland*, ed. by Stephen Paget (1921), p. 268.

Flood. The right way to understand this mythology, to which I want to direct attention first of all, is not to try to trace these stories back along the course of history to some chronologically prehistoric period, but to trace them down into the hidden depths of human existence as it always is; they are pointers, that is, to the fundamental nature of every man and of every society; they are not events that occurred once for all in a prehistoric period. The Fall in particular is to be traced not back along history but down into the hidden depths of human personality, of every human personality.

It is a deplorable fact that about a hundred years has been wasted theologically in ridiculous debates about whether the world was really created in six days, whether Adam and Eve actually existed, whether the serpent actually spoke, etc., etc. There are still people who try to perpetuate these arid debates among students. If it is necessary to join in them or to advert to them, then certainly we must say that the modernists were right and the fundamentalists were wrong in regard to the matters about which they differed. But in consequence of the absorption of attention by these unedifying and prosaic wrangles (when the Book of Genesis is in question) insufficient thought has been given to the profound truths which are enfolded in this mythology about the perennial data of historical existence.

I wonder how much of the superficiality or the triviality of the ordinary Englishman's notion of what is involved in historical existence is due to the failure of those who were commissioned to expound the Bible to instil into the common imagination the profundities of the Genesis mythology. A. N. Whitehead hazarded the prophecy 'that that religion will conquer which renders clear to popular understanding some eternal greatness incarnate in the passage of temporal fact'.[1]

[1] *Adventures of Ideas* (1938), p. 41.

The Bible does that from Genesis onwards—not least in Genesis.

The myth of the creation of man by God means that mankind is not self-derived, self-explanatory, or self-sufficing. Mankind derives its existence from God, that is, from the eternal Being who is the fount and origin of historical existence, as well as its last end. Human existence can be explained and has meaning only with reference to God and God's purpose; man is so constituted that he never can become autonomous. Man is set between what is higher and lower than himself and he will be blessed only if he is in right relation with both the one and the other. Man is certainly part of nature; he is formed of the dust of the earth. But he is not merely part of nature; he transcends nature. He is made in the image of God, which cannot be said of nature, not even of the highest animals. Man's being is, as it were, suspended between God and nature and is linked to both. Man is a creature, and yet a creature who can hear God speak and who can consciously respond to and co-operate with God and rebel against God. If man were merely part of the flux of nature, his existence would have no special significance; his history is meaningful because of the special relation in which he stands to God.

That man is made in the image of God the Creator means also that he is called upon to share and to co-operate in the work of creation and under God is responsible for sustaining historical existence. Man is thus called by God to creative activity in domestic and political life, in art and craftsmanship, in technology and science, in industry and agriculture. These are all divinely ordained ways of participating in God's work of creating and preserving the world and drawing out its latent possibilities.

We take note then that the Bible, unlike many religious philosophies, does not regard man's earthly existence with its natural or material necessities as necessarily evil, although it is necessarily finite and limited. Nature in itself is good, and is not to be escaped from as far as possible or as quickly as possible. Man is not evil or diseased or astray because he is part of nature; the harmony that exists in the Garden of Eden before the Fall—harmony between God, man and nature— indicates that it is ideally possible that human existence, historical existence, should be harmonious, blessed, joyful. It is not because man is finite but because he is sinful that his history is a record of disease and discord and conflict. It is because man is a fallen being that historical existence is existence in exile. In history man is not at home with God as he ought to be, and as he could be despite his finitude. It is sin, not finitude, which causes God to be a hidden God to historical man. Adam before the fall is not historical man, but man as he might have been. The fallenness of man means that both the individual and the group (the nation, etc.) always in history seek to be self-sufficient; the sin of man has been well-described as 'god-almightiness'. It is beautifully epitomized in the saying of Napoleon II: 'If God gave me permission to address him a petition which he would fulfil, I should ask him to descend from his throne and let me occupy it.'[1] The tragedy of man is that this pretension to god-almightiness carries him out of the place in which alone he can be happy and at ease. All men and all civilizations—in the measure that they are creative and dynamic—try to make themselves absolute when in reality they cannot lift themselves above the dependence and relativity that have been assigned to them in virtue of their status as creatures. There is a power at work within us which is always fighting against the true law of our being. 'The doctrine of original sin points to the fact that in the very depth of the human spirit resides a tendency which betrays his

[1] Quoted by Dormer Creston, *In Search of Two Characters* (1945), p. 367.

manhood, which exposes him to the forces of disintegration and belies his true destiny'[1]

The stories at the beginning of the Book of Genesis are not then historical stories, like those we learn about Julius Caesar or William the Conqueror; they are stories not about this man or that, but about man himself; they are mythological stories which help us to understand the history of mankind at whatever point we turn to it or at whatever page we open it.

The story of the Flood or of the universal Deluge is a picture of the awful fate that man would bring upon himself if he were left to himself. If God left human egotism and pride, man's god-almightiness, to work out to its natural result—chaos, complete self-destruction, would be the end product. The earth would have been filled with violence, as Genesis says. That is what man, left to himself, would deserve and get—destruction. This is the only right of the natural man, the right to die.

But then there are no natural men, no men entirely left to themselves. The men who actually exist in history are those who have survived the flood, who are children of Noah; that is, men upon whom God has mercy, despite their sinful nature. 'His reasons of mercy (as an old writer said) are all drawn from himself, and not from anything in us.' Man exists, and continues to exist, not by his own right but by the mercy of God. In spite of the fact, in the words of Genesis, that 'the imagination of man's heart is evil from his youth', God has mercifully determined to preserve our historical existence. 'While the earth remaineth, seedtime and harvest, and summer and winter, and day and night, shall not cease.' That is to say, God has promised always to maintain a sufficient order in the world for the support of human life. Not a perfect order, but a sufficient order. While the earth remains, God will not allow it to fall into the complete chaos, confusion and barrenness that are

[1] E. Lampert, *The Apocalypse of History* (1948), p. 93.

symbolized by the deluge. This is not paradise regained; the paradise, which is carried about in the memory of the human race as a lost possibility, cannot be regained in history. It never existed in history. But the conditions of historical existence are such as to allow man to hope for and even to anticipate the gift of paradise at the end of history. In regard to this, as we shall see, the new covenant illumines the old covenant.

Before leaving the myth of the flood, notice that it signifies more than that historical man is man preserved in existence by the mercy of God, despite the evil imagination of his heart. The myth of the descent of all men from Noah, from a single ancestor, like the myth of the descent of all men from Adam, signifies that despite all our diversities of race, colour, language, etc., in spite of our being in a state of contradiction and conflict with one another, we do all—originally and by the divine constitution of our race—belong together in one family. You might think that if you cease to believe the historicity of Noah, i.e., as a prehistoric patriarch, a common descent from him can no longer be regarded as a bond of human brotherhood, but the New Testament will show that the ground of the unity of mankind never was really or ultimately in Noah, nor even in Adam, but in Christ the Eternal Son, in whom God chose and looked upon mankind before the foundation of the world, and in whom the whole creation held together from the beginning. It is in the second Adam, not the first Adam, it is because of our relation to Christ, not to Noah, that we all originally belong together and can at last be restored into the unity of a family.

Those who accept Christ as the Head and bond of the human race, and who interpret human existence christologically, can reasonably say that the story of Noah foreshadows the truth that God is in a living relation to, is in communication with, all mankind, all nations, and not only with the seed of Abraham or with the children of Israel. Before the advent of Christ, the Bible could find no better way of saying this. In other words, the Bible knows from the outset that it is dealing with the universal history of mankind. So Genesis says that the sons of Noah who came out of the ark were Shem, Ham and Japheth—these three were the sons of Noah, and from them people spread over all the earth—and then a whole chapter is devoted to spreading out the descendants of Noah over the earth; thus a mere list of names may have more significance for 'History according to the Bible' than appears at first sight. The covenant that God establishes with Noah is a covenant with all mankind; the law that he gives to Noah is a sign that all mankind is given a divine law. The Noachian covenant and the Noachian law (as they have been called) mean that in principle the whole of mankind is in a covenant relationship to God and under a divine law. The special covenant with Israel and the law of the ten commandments are to be understood against that universal background. We are not true to the Bible if we confine God's dealings with men to his dealings with Israel. The Bible begins with the whole human race on the map, so to speak, and they are there all the way through even when they are not directly under observation.

Nevertheless, the Bible confessedly spot lights one special people, Israel—the Old Israel under the Old Covenant and the New Israel under the New Covenant, and we must now consider the relation between the history of Israel and the history of mankind. If we were not so accustomed to it, we should be scandalized by the fact that the Bible appears to represent God as favouring only one among all the nations of the world in the Old Testament, and only a select society, the Church, in the New Testament. There is no getting away from the fact that the God of the Bible does treat men and nations differently, not on any rational basis of equality that we can understand.

He appears to be highly selective and preferential. Is he then a God of favourites—a God who cares only for a sect or a section of mankind?

It must be admitted that the testimony of the Bible is not entirely free from ambiguity in this respect. You could cite a lot of texts in the Old Testament, and some in the New Testament, which on their face certainly imply that God is a God of favourites, and that he is arbitrary in his selection of those members of our race upon whom he confers privileges. There are elements in the Bible which might lead us to suppose that that is what God is like. But on the whole or at last this is not really the Biblical doctrine of election. Beneath the shrill treble of favouritism there sounds the deep bass note that the chosen people are chosen not for their own benefit but for the sake of all the nations of the earth.

The process of election begins with the call of Abraham; and it is to Abraham that God says: 'In thy seed shall all the nations of the earth be blessed.' All the way through the history of Israel these two interpretations of the divine election are struggling for supremacy, especially from the time of the exile onwards. The highest theme of prophecy was that Israel was chosen not for privilege but for service, to serve as the nucleus or centre for the gathering of all the nations round the throne of God. But it was terribly easy to treat this election as a ground for national pride and for a narrow exclusive conception of their national vocation. The question was this: was Israel chosen as the recipient of a special revelation of the will of God in order that it might witness to all other nations that they too were chosen and called into the Kingdom of God? Or was Israel chosen in order to show to other nations that they were *not* chosen, that they were *not* within the range of God's merciful purposes?

If there is any doubt about how we should answer this

question from the Old Testament, the New Testament makes it plain that the universal, all-embracing answer is the true one. Yet the history of the Church of Christ shows how easy it is to pervert the sense of election to service into the pride of election to exclusive privilege, for through a long period of its history churchmen have regarded with equanimity and even with gratification the consignment of all people outside the Church to everlasting perdition.

The ultimate theme both of Old Testament prophecy and of the gospel of the New Covenant is that God wills the salvation and reconciliation not of select individuals, not of one nation, not of the Church if the Church is taken to be only a section of humanity, but of all mankind and indeed of the whole cosmos. Nor does the gospel say only that God *wills* this, as though there were some doubt about whether he can accomplish what he wills—some doubt whether he can pull it off. God's Righteousness, to which the prophets of Israel constantly recur, does not signify a sort of passive attribute in God; it means the absolutely reliable activity of God by which he makes all things right. The Bible regards history as a dialectical movement, a conflict between good and evil, between divine and demonic powers, in which for long periods and even in the final cataclysm darkness may seem to prevail, but in which, when the clouds and darkness have cleared away, the last word will be found to be this triumphant all-embracing, all-transforming Righteousness of God. The Bible teaching about election and predestination must be interpreted in the context of the universal cosmic redemption which is the heart of the gospel. 'Grace and election are the mystery and the essence of history,' said Troeltsch.

It might seem to us that the gospel of God's righteousness and of the restoration of all things should have been immediately communicated to the whole race indiscriminately; that the Holy Spirit should have been poured out all at once on the whole race and that all mankind should at once have been overtly drawn into the kingdom of God. Was there any real need for the process, to which the Bible bears witness, of the communication of the word of God and the Spirit of God here and there to special individuals, to a special family, a chosen people? All the Bible can say is that this is how God has chosen to work out the redemption of the world. He uses human means; but why he elects to use this means and not that, this man and not that, this nation and not that, this institution and not that, is a mystery which we cannot penetrate.

But there is this to be said; this is the way in which things do work in this world. It might appear to us that it would be more equitable and rational if, for example, new discoveries in medicine and surgery had become known at once to the general mind of the race and so have been at once available everywhere and for all; but it never has been so. In every respect blessings that eventually reach all the nations of the world come first through 'chosen' individuals or groups. We cannot explain why this should be so. The doctrines of divine election and predestination are a way of saying that God has so ordered and constituted the world, and so it must be all right, in spite of the appearance of arbitrariness and lack of equity that is entailed.

But according to the Bible within the whole dialectical process of history *every* nation is chosen, and every individual, to do something in working out the divine purpose. If the Lord brought up Israel out of Egypt, he also brought the Philistines from Caphtor and the Syrians from Kir, and he has designs for Assyria and Egypt. Cyrus as well as David is a servant of the Lord, though the kind of work one is called to do is very different from that of the other, and one knows that he is chosen by God whereas the other serves God in ignorance of his Name. Even the Pharaohs of history, the Hitlers and the Stalins, in their very opposition to the divine purpose are still within the divine plan and purpose; in some mysterious sense it is he who hardens their hearts. This is no doubt incredibly mysterious; but it *is* after all a gospel; it does mean that God is God; he is sovereign over all, and man's mightiest misuse of his freedom, his rebellion against God, cannot carry him outside the range of the providential purposes of God.

Nevertheless, while there is a providential purpose and calling for every man and for every nation, yet obviously according to the Bible the choice and calling of the nation of Israel are significant for all men in a way that other elections were not. God's special dealings with Israel are of unique significance for mankind. They are an *édition de luxe* of his dealings with the race. The experience of Israel is one which enables all nations to read *their* calling, *their* responsibility, *their* rejection, and *their* restoration; 'All history', said Carlyle, 'is an inarticulate Bible,' and we might add as a rider that every nation is an inarticulate Israel.

First, there is the creation and preservation of the nation. Israel always looked back to the Exodus, their deliverance from bondage in Egypt, as the event which constituted them a nation and to which they owed their freedom. This means that every nation which receives the freedom of nationhood may look upon its existence as due to a liberating and creative act of God. A book has been written entitled *The Miraculous Birth of Language*; another might be written entitled *The Miraculous Birth of Nations*. Certainly, even apart from the plagues of Egypt, it is a miracle that the cowed slaves who escaped from Pharaoh's bondage became eventually such a nation as Israel was—and is. It is a miracle of mercy that men, being centres of conflicting egotism, should be entitled to live a free, common life together at all, whether in the family, the tribe, the nation, or any larger group. The Old Testament witness that Israel was called to be the people of God and a righteous nation is a sign to all other peoples that they too are called to be a people of God and a righteous nation, that they too should praise the mercy of God for their corporate existence, their several and distinct traditions and advantages. We are each to regard the events which brought our nation into existence and set us on our feet as a people with a common life and destiny— as analogous to the Exodus. We are each to regard our preservation in our native land as analogous to the preservation of Israel in the Holy Land, and our national ordeals as analogous to those of Israel. Our nation too, like Israel, has a work appointed for it to do and a witness to bear in history by the Lord of history. If we take all this in, we shall find our common life as a nation has a quality of mystery and a depth of meaning that we had not realized while we looked upon it as what is called merely 'secular': our national history becomes sacred history.

Secondly, while a nation owes to the liberating activity of God, its birth and its calling forth into distinct existence it also receives from him its law and constitution. Most of what the Pentateuch says about the delivery of the Law to Moses is of course aetiological; i.e. it was the way in Israel to trace back all *leges* and *mores* to institution by Moses, as it might be the way in England to attribute the origination of our laws and customs to Magna Carta. The point of this is that at every stage of its national development Israel acknowledged God as the ultimate author of its law and constitution. It was God who addressed the nation through the mediation of Moses and those who sat in Moses' seat. Moreover, Israel held in the end that the hard core of the law, namely the Ten Commandments, was God's law, not only for Israel but for mankind: the decalogue was universal in its obligation. There was a rabbinic legend that God originally spoke the Ten Commandments simultaneously in all the languages of the world. If nations today came to confess that their laws and constitution had at their core the authority of God and were a sign of their subjection to the throne of the universe, and were not just something they invented or what could be accounted for solely by economic determinism or what is changeable at pleasure without reference to the divine purpose for mankind, then a depth and a sanction and a magic would return to politics and jurisprudence that are at present lacking.

The book of Deuteronomy is a book of cardinal importance for the Old Testament interpretation of history. It was written somewhere around the end of the monarchy or the beginning of the exile. It is the most sustained and coherent proclamation and working out of Israel's vocation as a nation, a nation chosen to serve God in a pure and just common life. It insists again and again that God will bless and prosper Israel only if Israel obeys his commandments. The school of writers that compiled Deuteronomy, whom we call the Deuteronomists, also edited or re-edited the historical books in the Old Testament, in which this moral canon of judgment is applied throughout the history of Israel with a stern and indeed somewhat artificial vigour. According to this yardstick, the nation prospered when it did justly, and met with calamities when it was morally corrupt or idolatrous.

In their insistence on exclusive allegiance to the God of Righteousness and on the obligations of social justice, the Deuteronomists were of course applying the teaching of the great prophets; but their work was on a lower level than that of the prophets. Perhaps prophets who turn chroniclers are bound to lose something of their flair. According to the Deuteronomists, every king is dubbed either A1 or C3, by a much too simple test of piety. They try to make history much too tidy. Further, while they are sure that Jehovah is the God of the whole earth and supreme over all nations, yet according to them he is interested in the welfare of Israel alone; they do not, like some at any rate of the prophets, perceive the universal mission of Israel. Again, the message of the Deuteronomists, with its reiterated emphasis on obeying the commandments and statutes of the Lord, obviously prepared the way for the extravagant legalism which may have been the strength but was also the fatal weakness of Israel after the Exile. The impression left by Deuteronomy is that the divine election is to national privilege, not to universal service. The privileges of election will be received only if the people serve Jehovah, but there is no suggestion that God's purpose in election embraces all nations.

It was the prophets, not the chroniclers or the scribes, who perceived this.[1] It was the prophets through whom new insights came. It was they also who wrestled on Israel's behalf with the problem of suffering; the mysterious fact that in history it is not infrequently the wicked—whether wicked men or wicked nations—that prosper and the righteous that are tormented. The Deuteronomists were not oppressed by this problem; on the other hand, it could only be felt as a problem when the elementary principles asserted by Deuteronomy had been accepted as axiomatic, namely that the world is built on moral foundations and that in the long run it is well with the good and ill with the wicked. If there is no God over history who demands righteousness and underwrites it, then there could be no *problem* of suffering. Out of the wrestling with this mystery we get not only the sublime poem Job, but the revolutionary and pregnant insight of the Servant Songs in Isaiah with their promise of a faithful Remnant who give

[1] In this essay I say less about the prophets than about other parts of the Bible but at the Conference, for which it was prepared, Biblical prophecy was being studied separately.

themselves to God's purpose of redemption by vicarious suffering—a promise which was very imperfectly realized in the history of Israel itself but pointed forward to the way in which God's Only Son and Righteous Servant would take upon himself all the burden and disease of historical existence and so redeem and transfigure it.

But the Old Testament only hints at this; all it does at last is to show how easily in history good things go bad, and how history itself raises an immense question, an awful dilemma . . . how for example a high regard for law and ethical conduct turns into the unlovely spectacle and predicament of legalism; how a conviction of being bound to God and wholly dependent on him may turn into the pride of being the exclusive favourites of God. Thus the Old Testament shows all peoples the characteristic impasses which historical existence produces. The New Testament, we shall see, does not show us a way out of or a way of avoiding these impasses, but it proclaims that God has a way of overcoming the insolubilities of history. The Christ says to those who believe in him 'in the world ye shall have tribulation', but he also says, 'Be of good cheer, I have overcome the world'.

II

I have said nothing so far about the Psalms as windows through which we may look into history as the Bible looks into it. In the Bible as well as in the Church the *lex orandi* is often the best way of finding your way into the *lex credendi*. A people's spontaneous forms of prayer reveal their deepest insights better than their laboured essays in thought. Consider, for example, Psalm 90:

Lord, thou hast been our dwelling place in all generations.
Before the mountains were brought forth,
    Or ever thou hadst formed the earth and the world,
Even from everlasting to everlasting, thou art God.

The Bible knows that at the back of history, both undergird-
ing it and overarching it, is the Eternal, the Lord God. There
is a dwelling place for man in history despite the apparent
homelessness, the terrible restlessness, the hopeless lack of
stability, in historical existence. It is this conviction that they
have their dwelling-place in God that prevents the men of the
Bible from trying to escape from history or from committing
suicide, out of sheer hopelessness or ennui. They know as well
as any Greek tragedian the transitoriness, the desolating frailty,
of our human existence.

Thou crumblest men away, summoning men back to the dust.
For a thousand years in thy sight are but as yesterday
    when it is past, and as a watch in the night.

In the end history doesn't seem to add up to anything; you
can't even call history a day: it is like three hours' sleep in the
dark.

But historical existence is not only transitory and frail; it is
sinful and guilty and subject to the wrath of God.

For we are consumed in thine anger
and in thy wrath we are troubled.
Thou dost expose our sins and layest our guilty secrets bare.

Up to a point or over certain stretches we can put up what
looks like a pretty good show in history but at the heart of it
is guilt, the guilt of pride, the guilty secret of historic existence.

Our days (our greatest days) droop in thy displeasure,
Our life is over like a sigh.

So there is no possibility of real fulfilment here. 'Swift as a
thought gay youth is past and gone.' This will strike our sanguine contemporaries as melancholy, but how much profounder it is than the shallow idealism of modern man who is
unable or afraid to look into the dark interior of history. We
could not, however, be melancholy about our transitoriness

and our guilt, did we not feel beyond it the eternity and the holiness of God. A sense of man's misery is tied to a sense of God's majesty. Modern man has lost both: we as modern men have lost both.

Notice that the melancholy, the pessimism, of the Bible never turns sentimental or morbid or cynical or fatalistic. The sense of transitoriness and of guilt that it awakens in us is, unlike many Victorian hymns, entirely wholesome. For melancholy of this sort, which keeps us aware of our real state, we should pray again and again.

> So teach us to number our days,
> That we may get a heart of wisdom

—a heart that manfully confesses the dark and guilty interior of historical existence. Then we can go on and pray:

> Relent, O Lord, and delay not,
> be sorry for thy servants,
> O satisfy us in the morning with thy mercy.

When we have been given that wise grace to come to terms with our transitoriness and our guilt, then no longer is it needful for us to be kept down in the dark by the wrath of God. God can now relent; the morning can come; there are after all open to us glorious satisfactions in history itself; it is possible even that we should rejoice and be glad now all our days; but only if God's work appears unto his servants—

> Let thy servants see thee at thy saving work,
> and let their children see thy glorious power.

If God is revealed at work within the conditions of our transitoriness, then indeed our existence will be given a sure hope and our guilt will be redeemed. Then indeed we can pray that the work of our hands, what we create in our civilizations, may be established. So far as it depends just on ourselves it is purely transitory and doomed, but if after all God the Eternal is at work in our history, transfiguring its death into life, then no moment or element of achievement in history need be finally lost. Thus the psalm ends with what is in effect an expectant prayer for the coming of the Christ—

Let the beauty of the Lord our God be upon us,
And establish thou the work of our hands upon us;
Yea, the work of our hands establish thou it.

For we cannot establish it. We cannot: but he can. This is the promise of the Old Testament.

When we turn on to the New Testament we may be struck at first by a more acute and intense pessimism about the possibilities of historical existence than ever we found in the Old Testament. So far from God establishing the work of our hands, he seems to be rushing it to its total destruction.

'There seems', Dr Lampert has said, 'to be a strange but unmistakable note of pessimism and even bitterness which pervades the New Testament in regard to the affairs of human History. It points—not only in its apocalyptic visions but throughout its entire message—to a shattered world, to a universe that is rent asunder into fragments, or tottering to its ruin, or reserved unto fire against the day of judgment and perdition.'[1]

We must agree that that does appear to be the New Testament attitude to this world, though that it is so is frequently overlooked and preachers preach hopeful little sermons with the New Testament in their hands about the outlook for Western civilization if only we pull ourselves together, etc. While they may utilize texts from the New Testament they would be hard put to it to show that the New Testament in its main tenor shows much concern for the values of Western civilization or for any civilization at all. The implicit, and indeed explicit, perspective of the New Testament is that

[1] E. Lampert, *The Apocalypse of History* (1948), p. 160.

history is about to come to an end, and a very good thing too.

Thus if the New Testament stood alone we might be at a loss to show that the Bible has anything positive and favourable to say about civilization or about the values of historical existence. But then the New Testament does not stand alone; it is inconceivable that it should stand alone. The New Testament presupposes the Old Testament with which it is rightly bound up in the literal sense, because it is bound up with it in every other sense as well. And, as we have already seen, the Old Testament has a great deal positively to say about history. This is carried over into the New Testament which does not wash out what the Old Testament says, but rather goes on from there and unveils still more of the mystery of historical existence. Broadly speaking, the New Testament takes for granted all that the Old Testament says, except where it definitely corrects the Old Testament, as in the case of the obligation to observe the Jewish ceremonial law. When this is appreciated, we may find that after all the New Testament opens up an understanding of history which is congruous with, and complementary to, that of the Old Testament and which brings us nearer still to the place of understanding.

There is also this to be said. Even if the New Testament writers had a lot they would have liked to say about civilization and the value of political and cultural activity, the circumstances in which the documents of the New Testament were written were not such as to call or provide scope for, that kind of subject. The Christians, for whom and to whom the New Testament was written, were a tiny minority in the society of the Roman Empire, eagerly trying to get a footing for their mission, all their energies absorbed in that. Even if their message had been one that anticipated the indefinite continuation of history, instead of being cast as it was in the mould of eschatological expectation, they were not in a position to assume political responsibilities or cultural leadership in the Empire, and they would have been historical absentees and quite unrealistic if they had concerned themselves with responsibilities that were not open to them and, so far as they could tell, never would be open to them. Their office was to insert into history—urgently, swiftly, with the utmost concentration—the gospel of the final things—they left over for a future, which they were not even in a position to anticipate, the bearing of this gospel on an historical existence that was to continue indefinitely.

It may be that this gospel, which deals with the absolutes rather than with the relativities of historical existence, which deals with the final rather than with the secondary decisions that men have to take, could be adequately set forth, be set on its course, and get its finality recognized, only at one of those dark periods in history when civilization seemed to be tottering. 'The fulness of the time' when the Christ came did not mean that history was ripe for a great move forward in its evolutionary process and progress—it meant that history had come to such an impasse that the time was apt for proclaiming what alone in the end gives history meaning, and what alone makes civilization worth while—what at last will be seen to be the goal or consummation for which all the history before and after the advent of the Christ was making. We can see in this sense that the fulness of the time had come so far as Judaism was concerned. Judaism had reached an impasse. A nation with a universal mission had become a narrow and exclusive sect; the Law, the Torah, with which it had been entrusted, and in which it had been intended to delight, had been corroded into an intolerable legalism (see St Paul's Epistle to the Romans); the fall of Jerusalem which was impending was the fitting symbol of the condition of Judaism.

Although on the face of it the prospect of the Roman Empire and the Hellenistic culture looked much brighter, we can see now that beneath the surface the seeds of decay and mortal sickness were already present. The Greco-Roman civilization has been described as a 'world decaying for lack of God and social morality'. As compared with the great days of the Republic there was a failure of nerve and a lowering of moral tone, a revival of superstition and astrology, fatalism, confusion of belief, unsureness and a consequent craving for security. All these things spell the coming of a dark night of civilization; but perhaps it was only up against a dark night that the final gospel of the judgment and mercy of God and of the eschatological transformation of all things could be heard and seen in its full power and glory. God discovereth deep things out of darkness, Job says. Civilization and culture are not the deepest things to be discovered in historical existence; perhaps they have to be threatened and imperilled when the hour is due for the discovery or the rediscovery of the deepest things of all.

We can see also a providential reason why the New Testament should not be too positive about any form of civilization: if it had been, the idea that the gospel permanently requires that particular civil polity would be sanctioned and that would be fatal. We know how ecclesiastics of various traditions have tried to found their favourite form of church order and government in the New Testament, though not with much success except in their own estimation. Happily there is not enough in the New Testament to tempt the politicians also to become archaeological.

The remarkable thing is that, despite the consuming occupation of the Apostolic Church with eschatology whether realized, or futurist, or both, the New Testament is far from being completely world-renouncing. The apostolic testimony certainly affirms the political order in very high terms; and, though it undoubtedly sets them against a new background, it does affirm the virtues of civilized life. There is in the New Testament a genuine concern for the civic and social virtues, though the inculcation of these is neither the heart of the gospel nor the chief burden of the apostolic preaching. The ethical codes which were commonplaces in the Hellenistic world are reproduced in the New Testament and so are baptized. The New Testament after all contains the Epistle of St James as well as the Epistles of St Paul, and the Epistle to the Romans contains Chapters 12 following as well as Chapters 1-11. And although the deepest things of the gospel are in Chapters 1-11, the rest are also there and are an essential part of the picture. But what are some of the deep things about historical existence that are discovered in the New Testament?

The advent of Jesus the Christ was not only *one* of those events, after which it *may* be said, 'Things can never again be the same,' but the Event, after which it *must* be said, 'Things can never again be the same.' The measure in which that can be said is the criterion of the historic importance of any event. I remember very many years ago hearing someone say that you might agree or you might disagree with Bergson, but that your thinking could never be the same again after you had read him. If the reading of certain books can be climacteric, still more so can the undergoing of certain experiences. Really to experience the advent of Jesus the Christ is the climacteric experience of all history. But alas, it is exceedingly difficult for us to experience the advent. In Christendom we have all been educated to take the advent of Jesus the Christ for granted—to take it for granted!! Even if we have not had what is called 'a Christian education', even if we have received no instruction in what is called 'religious knowledge', we have at least been taught to date events B.C. and A.D. That is to say, we assume as a matter of course that there is something that pulls history together, gives it a pattern, prevents it from being a monotonous or meaningless flux, and gives it a central point of reference. It is almost impossible for us to imagine what history would be like—a history in which there never had been and never would be any event of epoch-making importance or of *aeon*-making importance. In this quite elementary sense the advent of Jesus the Christ does pull history together, and gives us a point of reference whatever we make of it— even if we can make nothing of it, or even if we protest against it.

But secondly the advent is not just an historical event, an event *within* history; it is not even the greatest historical event. It is not, as it were, an extraordinary event that emerges out of the midst of history in the ordinary course of events, and dominates it simply like the highest peak in a mountain range. The advent of Jesus the Christ can of course be looked at like that. But if you look long enough at it and try to take in its intrinsic meaning—what it has to say for itself—instead, that is, of trying to fit it into a scheme which you have already got in your mind—you come to see that the advent, if it means anything, means everything. It means that history has once for all been touched, embraced, broken, ravished, conquered and transformed by the Eternal. In the advent God and man, eternity and time, were once for all completely engaged. If history can be summed up (as it has been) as 'the inter-action of God and man'—it is in the advent of Christ, the God-man, that it has been so summed up, not merely by way of a definition but in conclusive and irrevocable Act. History is no longer promiscuous, it has been indissolubly married. Every part of it has once for all had immortal worth conferred on it.

Here, says Dr Lampert, 'we are brought to a point in which a unique divine-human event—the Incarnation—has occurred, thus revealing a new meaning and a new dimension in

History. When we find ourselves in this new dimension, every fragment of Time, every period of History—every man, every nation, every state, every civilization, every human activity—are shown to stand in an immediate relation to God: they exist in their peculiar and unrepeatable situations as an inalienable part of that great movement of which Christ is the *Alpha* and *Omega*, the Beginning and the End.'[1]

If that is true, then indeed the advent of Jesus the Christ was the Event in the light of which nothing can ever be the same again, and in the light of which we see how things were from the beginning, and what they are leading up to in the end. Let us try to see what it is that the advent of Christ established as regards historical existence—assuming that he is what he claimed to be and what the New Testament proclaims him to be.

First, by being made flesh he has proved once for all that the flesh is not inherently or wholly evil; else he, the All-Holy One, could not have been made flesh. By becoming incarnate in the historical, that is, in the realm of the finite, the limited, the relative, the changing, he has shown that this realm, however much it has been perverted by sin, is nevertheless capable of being redeemed, and indeed has been redeemed, so that God can be obeyed and glorified in the flesh. The New Testament is emphatic in its rejection of what is called 'Docetism', that is the doctrine that the flesh is inherently evil and therefore Jesus cannot really have been incarnate, but his appearance in a body must have been only an appearance. We have not to flee from the finite, or to escape from the flesh, or to seek to be mystically elevated above it. It is in the flesh, in the relativities of historical existence, that all who accept Christ as Lord and Master will seek to obey and glorify God.

[1] Lampert, op. cit., p. 32.

Secondly, in his proclamation, in his Evangel, Jesus confirmed and ratified the prophetic testimony of the Old Covenant to God's purpose and ways in history. He came not to destroy but to fulfil the Law and the Prophets. Indeed in his life of perfect obedience and holiness, and in his sacrifice of himself even to the death of the Cross, the meaning and message of the Law and the Prophets were perfectly embodied as they never had been in Israel. The word and the deed were at last completely one.

But thirdly, the relation of Jesus to the history that preceded His advent is ambivalent. He confirms that in it and through it God had been speaking and acting. History was the field in which God was establishing his sovereignty and confronting sinful men with the claims of his Kingdom in judgment and in mercy, with Israel as his chosen instrument. But, in confirming that, Jesus showed the hopeless unfitness of Israel or of any other earthly historical society or institution to incorporate the Kingdom. In fact, when the Kingdom of God was embodied in history in Jesus himself, Israel along with Greece and Rome was the instruments of his rejection. Jesus thus showed that though God has never been estranged from the world, or has never left the world without witness, the world had become so estranged from God that it did not even recognize him as God when he came to be the last word both in judgment and in mercy. Or perhaps we should say that men recognized him only too well but would not admit that they did so. For the crucifixion is the coming to a head of man's universal protest against God, the protest against God that there is in all of us, the will that there be no God, the will that we be or make our own gods.

'Christ was the supreme challenge to all the forces of darkness in the world; at all costs he must be destroyed; Herodians and Pharisees must forget their enmity; Pharisees and

Sadducees must for once co-operate; Judah must work hand in hand with Rome. . . . Like a magnet he drew upon himself all the forces and reserves of evil; he compelled them to a supreme and final test.'[1] They nailed him to the cross, they drove him to death—death which is the sign of the vanity and dissolution that lie over all historical existence. He went right through history to that.

The Resurrection of Christ was, however, the sign that death is not what it appears to be, that history does not end in dissolution, that God can recreate and transfigure historical existence and take it up into the Eternal Order. The risen victorious Life of Christ and of the redeemed race in Christ is a resurrection, a transfiguration; that is to say, there is continuity between historical life and eternal life; it does not mean the replacement of what has existed in history by something entirely different. All the fragmentary and obscure realizations in history of the glory and of the Kingdom of God will be taken up and fulfilled in Eternity. The taking up of historical existence into heaven in the ascension of Christ is the sign that all things here, when they have been purged, will be taken up into the New Creation.

He ascended far above all heavens that he might fill all things. He has already begun to fill all things. He is now where he has the freedom of the universe. It was said of Henry Scott Holland that 'he was like sunshine filling a room and bringing out every spark of colour latent in it'.[2] So, the ascended Christ is like sunshine filling the universe, and bringing out every spark of colour latent everywhere. His filling of all things, his transfiguring of all things, is going on already behind the scenes; we see little bits and sparkles of this work of his which break through here on earth, but until the last day his filling

[1] Nathaniel Micklem, *The Doctrine of our Redemption* (1943), pp. 44f.
[2] Paget, op. cit., p. vii.

of all things is hidden and incomplete; indeed still subject to opposition and interference from the powers of evil. All the same, the eye of faith, illuminated by the Holy Spirit, can already see signs of Christ's presence everywhere and can a little anticipate what his filling of all things, when it is unveiled, will be like.

Nevertheless, the New Testament which tells us that he ascended far above all heavens that he might fill all things, and so encourages us already to look for marks of his presence in all things, does not look at the world, as it is now, through romantic or mystical eyes. It says, what is obvious: 'As it is we do not yet see everything in subjection to him.' It is only Jesus so far that we see crowned with glory and honour, and it is by faith alone that we see him so crowned. Christ's reign over the world is at present so hidden and mysterious that we are often tempted to conclude that it is the devil or the demons who reign, and not he. That history is a battle-ground between divine and demonic forces is nowhere more plainly asserted than in the New Testament; nevertheless, the New Testament is a gospel, is good news, because it proclaims that however awful the conflict, however deadly the disorder and the pride which we feel and see both in the world at large and in ourselves, yet it is the Lord Christ who is really on the throne of the universe and his kingly rule will at last prevail over all things as it prevails already at the heart of things.

It is a solemn and fortifying thought that interior to all space, time and history there is a world where God's name is perfectly hallowed, his will fully done, and his Kingdom already come. . . . To have faith unhinged by what we now see is to confess that it was a faith unfounded and unfed from the eternal source (P. T. Forsyth).

In the advent of Christ the foundation and the food of this faith came forth from the eternal source, and in every eucharist

believers are taken to that foundation and that place of nourish-
ment.

The outpouring of the Spirit, to which page after page of the
New Testament bears witness (and page after page of church
history too), is the breaking through into historical existence
of the beginnings of Christ's work of cosmic renewal and
transformation. Wherever men wait upon Christ with peni-
tent faith and expectancy (like the apostles in the upper room)
the Holy Spirit who renews the earth, i.e. nature, is able also
to renew history. In the apostolic age this renewal of life, not
only of personal life, but of the shared life and work of a
community, *koinonia*, was the cardinal experience of believers
and the visible outcome of the advent of Jesus. Though at the
time there was, as we have seen, no expectation that Pentecost
and its immediate sequel would lead to a renewal of civilization, yet the seeds of a new civilization were then being sown.
The promise contained in the second chapter of the Acts of the
Apostles, where on the day of Pentecost representatives of all
the nations are symbolically represented as hearing the good
news of the universal salvation in their own language, that is,
in the medium of their own culture, this promise was fulfilled
and is still being fulfilled. Mark also how St Paul could exclaim
to the Corinthians, 'All things are yours', when nothing could
have appeared to be further from the truth. 'All things are
yours'—a passage which is by itself the charter of Christian
culture.

For this is the amazing thing that although the face of the
New Testament if you look at it from one angle is autumnal . . .
the leaves are falling, the end of all things is at hand, it is the
last hour: yet look again and say whether at any moment in
history there was ever such spring in the air, such sap rising,
such a season of refreshing, such recreative work going on, the
singing of new songs, the giving of new names, the moulding

of a new vocabulary for the authentic conveyance of the new experience and the new possibility that had come into the world, the setting of new problems, the tasting of new powers, the raising of ineffable new hopes and expectations. Or, to put the case more moderately and concisely, the New Testament shows, in the words of an American theologian, how it is that 'In God's Kingdom on earth we taste delights which only in heaven can be complete, and in our service of God and man on earth raise problems which only heaven can solve' (E. R. Hardy).

What we really need to know is whether according to the Bible historical existence, life in this world, what we do in history and what we make of history, has any ultimate, permanent, intrinsic meaning and value. In other words, does God care intimately about culture and civilization, about politics and the struggle for social power? Or does he, like many latter day Christians, really care intimately and passionately only about the salvation of individuals and about the Church considered as quite distinct from, and infinitely superior to, the civilizations with which it happens to be mixed up? Are this world and its history in the last resort just incidental scenery for the drama of testing and saving souls? Is it the souls that come out of history and are rescued from the world that alone matter in the end, and would any other stage or scenery do just as well? Are all civilizations, are all historical conditions fundamentally as good or as bad as each other?

'There are happily still people who ask [wrote P. T. Forsyth] what all the long and tragic train of history means, what great thing does it intend, what destiny is it moving to, where its close shall be. To what do all things work together? They ask what is it all worth at last, what is to be the end of earth's long historic day. Is it sheer oblivion or another morning? Has history a destiny worth all its awful cost? Do all its large lines converge on anything, its throbbing sorrows, its soaring aspirations, its tragedies sordid or sublime, its dreadful conflicts, its splendid achievements, its miserable failures, its broken hearts and ruined civilisations, its conquests over nature and its collapses into it—do they all curve in some vast trend and draw together to a due close?'[1]

There can be no doubt about the Old Testament answer to these questions. History has a destiny and a goal; the Lord will create a new heaven and a new earth, and his people will be glad and rejoice for ever in that which he creates: and there is no suggestion of any radical discontinuity between history and the Kingdom to come. Even if the perspective of the New Testament is at first sight different—even if Christians and Christian orthodoxy have to a large extent thought that it allowed or commanded them to regard conditions in this world as a matter of indifference, yet the New Testament at bottom certainly regards this world and its history as something more than a stage on which personalities are fashioned for the Eternal Kingdom after which the stage is entirely discarded and done with. The Eternal Kingdom of God will not be merely saints subsisting in some sort of disembodied relationship with one another; the Kingdom will be a new world; there will be a world, a transformed and reconciled world, in the Kingdom of God. In some mysterious way both nature and history are to be taken up into the final consummation; therefore all that we do with nature and in history is of ultimate importance and of eternal moment. The Lord's promise to create a new heaven and earth, to make all things new—the Old Testament promise that is reiterated in the New Testament —while obviously passing what we can understand—implies the transfiguration—not the negation or destruction—of the natural and the historical. The great theme of resurrection

[1] P. T. Forsyth, *The Justification of God* (1916), pp. 224f.

implies the same. Not least significant is St Paul's statement that 'the creation itself will be set free from its bondage and obtain the glorious liberty of the children of God'.

Remember also that the story of the Transfiguration of our Lord lies firmly embedded in the gospel story, even if we hardly know what to make of it, and in Western Christendom have not tried to make much of it. 'And yet', as F. D. Maurice said, 'the Transfiguration has lived on through ages, and has shed its light upon all ages. . . . In the light of that countenance *which was altered, of that raiment which was white and glistering,* all human countenances have acquired a brightness, all common things have been transfigured. A glimpse of the divine beauty has broken through the darkness.'[1] The Archbishop of York concludes his book on the Transfiguration by speaking of 'the Christian faith not as a panacea of progress nor as an other-worldly solution unrelated to history, but as a gospel of Transfiguration. Such a gospel (he says) both transcends the world and speaks to the immediate here-and-now. He who is transfigured is the Son of Man; and, as he discloses on Mount Hermon another world, he reveals that no part of created things and no moment of created time lies outside the power of the Spirit, who is Lord, to change from glory to glory.'[2]

But as the disciples were not allowed to tarry on the Mount or to speak of what they had seen, so the New Testament does not encourage us to speculate about the manner of the ultimate transfiguration of nature and history, nor does it entrance us with mystic contemplations of the glory that shall be revealed. The disciples had to go down the mountain to deal with the hard case of the epileptic boy. The way to the glory that shall be revealed is the way of sacrificial action in the turmoil of

[1] F. D. Maurice, *The Gospel of the Kingdom of Heaven* (1893), pp. 157f.
[2] A. M. Ramsey, *The Glory of God and the Transfiguration of Christ* (1949), p. 147.

history, 'mucking in' as we crudely put it, the way of the cross; historical existence is a way to life through death. Therefore the New Testament never pauses for long over its moments of ecstasy, but at once rubs our noses again in our calling to obedience to the will of God and to the service of the neighbour in the here and now.

But as the believer makes his way along the narrow path of obedience, or as he follows the Lord at a great distance along the way of the cross, ever and again he may be allowed glimpses of the transfiguration that is to be—in the beauty of nature, in the face of a child, in the courage of an unpopular statesman, in those who tend the sick and support the aged and serve the poor in hidden out-of-the-way places where they have no chance of becoming popular. There are moments like this which take your breath away, but only moments.

The New Testament is extraordinarily realistic about this. It judges and saves and draws you into a world and a way of life where the glory that is to transfigure all things is always and already there, but it is still beneath the surface, behind the veil; and on the surface, this side of the veil, there is still what seems like an infinity of turmoil and conflict and shame. For what you actually see and feel, what you have to cope with here and now, is a little corner of the great battlefield between the divine and demonic forces which will continue so long as history lasts, and in this warfare, both without and within, it is God's will that you should be continually engaged. The New Testament contains formidable warnings about this warfare; not only will it continue until the final unveiling of the Son of God, but the demonic forces, the powers of evil, may appear to be winning and even victorious just before the end. That is to say, the New Testament prepares the believer for the worst as well as for the best, for the worst before the best. It does not speak to us of a good time coming in some future period of history; it says nothing about progress. The gospel settles your confidence not in the future but in the Eternal. The faith that overcomes the world has an altogether stronger note and an altogether surer object than any idealism that you can think of. In the words of P. T. Forsyth, the gospel—

> was not the hope of a conquering Messiah soon. 'He is here', was the Gospel. And so we are not hopeful that the world will be overcome; we know it has been. We are born into an overcome, a redeemed world. To be sure of that changes the whole complexion of life, religion and action in a way to which today we are strange. It is much to be quite sure that the world will one day be righteous; it is more to know that a universal Christ is its perfect righteousness already. We see not yet all things put under righteousness, but we see Jesus already crowned with that glory and honour. That is Christianity.[1]

Unless that conviction is reborn in us there is little prospect of our finding a meaning in the history of our time or of all time; and there is no prospect at all of our engaging in the conflicts and enterprises of history with that stedfast conviction and that carefree abandon which characterized the faith and action of the men of the apostolic age. But let this conviction be reborn and then it may be proved once more that the men who get most purchase on history and do most to change its course are not those who look forward either to a future period of history or to a next world which has no relation to this world: but the men who have already experienced the Advent and who believe in that Age to Come which is not just another period of history but the Age which is at·once beyond all history and is nevertheless already present in history at every point, above all at every moment and at every place of decision, in every opportunity of response.

[1] Forsyth, op. cit., pp. 228f.

V

HOLY WORLDLINESS[1]

You will feed with pleasure upon everything that is His. So that the world shall be a grand Jewel of Delight unto you: a very Paradise and the gate of Heaven. It is indeed the beautiful frontispiece of eternity; the Temple of God, and Palace of His Children.—Thomas Traherne

A BAD workman is said to complain of his tools, and it may be that only a bad speaker complains of the title of his allocution. My title for this occasion— 'Christian Sanctification faced with "the World"'— was given to me, and when I came to address myself to it I found it neither elegant nor pointed—nor intriguing. A good title ought, I think, to have at least one of those characters, unless of course it is one of those immense and magnificent eighteenth-century titles that tell you everything you want to know. While I hope I am going to speak about what I am supposed to be going to speak about, I will by your leave provide myself with a title that is certainly briefer and to my mind better. I am going then to speak about 'Holy Worldliness'.

The words 'world' and 'worldly' are in themselves morally neutral. As Newman said, 'by the world is very commonly meant the present visible system of things, without taking into consideration whether it is good or bad'.[2] 'Worldly', though it has acquired a predominantly pejorative sense, was originally synonymous with 'mundane', and when a bridegroom says to a bride, 'With all my worldly goods I thee endow', the word still bears this meaning. Indeed, it was retained in this sense in the Revised Prayer Book of 1928, although the sentiment of the proposition was modernized by substituting the

[1] A lecture to the Church Union School of Sociology at Oxford on 30 July 1956.

[2] J. H. Newman, *Parochial and Plain Sermons*, vi. 28.

notion of 'sharing' for that of 'endowing'. I must allow that according to the *New English Dictionary* the use of 'worldliness' in a morally neutral sense is rare to the point of obsolescence, and this noun on Christian lips has nearly always a very unfavourable connotation. But I should like to redeem it and to rescue it from monopolization by the devil. At least, I want to reflect upon the fact that the world was both created and redeemed in Christ. Since that is so, it should be possible and right to speak of a 'holy' as well as of an 'unholy' worldliness.

To avoid any initial misunderstanding I will to try to indicate in a few words what 'unholy worldliness' is, and then I trust you will not suspect me of condoning it. There is no question in my mind that 'unholy worldliness' is a very bad thing. But when we say that so-and-so is 'worldly'—in a pejorative sense, what exactly do we, or what ought we to, mean? Or when we accuse ourselves of 'worldliness'—which is doubtless a more salutary, though a less common, exercise—which of our many deplorable proclivities ought we to have in mind? To be worldly in this bad sense is to conform uncriticially and complacently to the standards and fashions that prevail in the earthly society of which one is inevitably a member. Cardinal Manning said that a man who is trying to serve two masters is a worldly man, and worldly men may be said to try to serve both God and mammon, if in their time and place it is a social convention to acknowledge God as well as to serve mammon. It is to be supposed that they do not make much of a job of the service of God, and so the emphasis here should be placed upon the service of mammon.

Worldly men have their hearts set on the things of this world—for example, money, success, or power—and seek them not as means but as ends. Their treasure is on earth, and *not in heaven*: to the exclusion, that is, of any real reference to all that heaven signifies. To put it in another way, worldly men not only 'belong' here—in the world, which in my view is a good thing to do; but they do not belong anywhere else. They are not held or haunted by anything beyond the present visible system of things. They have no sense of another world on the threshold of which the men of this world are always living. There is in their estimation (whatever conventional professions they may make) no unseen realm of mystery with a weight of glory—or at least heavy with enigmas. It has been said of Herbert Spencer that he 'was *not* an otherworldly man. Poetry, mystery, imagination, played no part whatever in his life'.[1] Exactly. All the investments of worldly men, whether for themselves or for other people, are in what is tangible, and they are always either rationally or instinctively calculating where these tangible interests lie.

Those who (thus) love the world, those who surrender themselves to it [as F. D. Maurice said] never understand it, never in the best sense enjoy it; they are too much on the level of it—yes, too much below the level of it . . . to be capable of contemplating it and of appreciating what is most exquisite in it. . . . The world . . ., though altogether good to the man who refers it to a Father, is the provocative of all evil in him when it becomes separated from his Father, and is substituted for Him.[2]

But I hardly need to say more about 'unholy worldliness'. Unless you live on quite a different plane from that which I inhabit, you know all too well what it is in yourself. I do not want in any way to mitigate the severity with which we judge ourselves in this regard. On the other hand, I do not want our just reprobation of unholy worldliness to blind us to our vocation to holy worldliness.

Perhaps we should seek to be at least approximately agreed about what we mean by 'the world', in the context of our

[1] Noel Annan, *Leslie Stephen* (1951), p. 154.
[2] F. D. Maurice, *The Epistles of St. John* (1881), pp. 124-7; cp. *Lincoln's Inn Sermons*, ii. 109.

present discussions. In the Bible, in ecclesiastical parlance, and in general usage, this word 'the world' bears a tiresome variety of meanings and shades of meaning. Sometimes the meaning is determined by that with which 'the world' is contrasted. I possess, or used to possess, a book entitled *Twelve Years in a Monastery* by Joseph McCabe, and it might be said that after those twelve years he returned to the world. Here the meaning is plain enough; living outside the cloister is contrasted with living inside. But at other times when the world is contrasted with something else the meaning is far from plain. 'The Church' and 'the world' are often contrasted or correlated, and in this case I am seldom happy about what is meant or implied. For it often seems to be implied that the Church is quite separable or distinguishable from the world, or that it is a section or corner of the world which is in the light in contrast to the rest which is in the dark. If I were myself going to speak in such terms, I should wish to say that the Church and the world are at least coterminous, or that the world is that part of the Church that has not yet come to its right mind. Père de Lubac, speaking of the Fathers of the Church, has pointed out that 'however far their gaze travelled, they could discern the *Corpus Ecclesiae* already in process of formation. For them, in fact, in a certain sense the Church was nothing else than the human race itself, in all the phases of its history, in so far as it was to lead to Christ and be quickened by his Spirit. It was the *omnis humana conditio*.'[1] Similarly, Maurice said that 'the Church . . . is a witness to all mankind of what God has done for them, and what they really are, created in Christ, and redeemed by Christ, and capable, but for their disbelieving this truth, and not taking their position as members of his body, of showing forth his character and his glory.'[2]

[1] H. de Lubac, *Catholicism* (Eng. trans., 1950), p. 93.
[2] F. D. Maurice, *Christmas Day* (1892), p. 180.

However, I do not wish to become involved in a discussion of philological niceties, and so I will content myself with endeavouring to specify positively what I mean here by 'the world'. I mean by 'the world' not only all that is visible and tangible, all the physical and psychic vitalities—what is commonly called by a conjunction of two multiguous words 'the world of nature'—but also the world of culture or of civilization that is, all that is specifically human, the works of intelligence and imagination (science and the arts), industry and agriculture, and all social and political institutions.

The question is sometimes posed whether by the Christian faith we are committed to renouncing or to affirming the world. Of course, if by the world is meant all that I have just named, it is impossible to renounce it absolutely and to go on living. World-renunciation must mean that we should be as lightly as possible attached to the things of the world and especially that we should eschew its pleasures. It is said of Sir James Stephen (Leslie Stephen's father) that he 'was inexorably suspicious of pleasure. He drank little; ate the lightest of meals; and asking himself once why it was that he continued to take snuff and receiving no satisfactory reply, ceremoniously emptied the box out of the window. "He once smoked a cigar," wrote Leslie, "and found it so delicious that he never smoked again." '[1] Is that a disposition towards the things of the world which we ought to regard as exemplary? Or, on the contrary, should we endorse the Jewish saying that 'a man will have to give account on the judgment-day of every good thing which he has refused to enjoy when he might have done so'?[2]

We must face the fact that at the most solemn moment in our lives (though most of us were unaware of it) we were pledged, apparently without qualification, 'to fight against . . .

[1] Annan, op. cit., p. 14.
[2] Quoted by K. E. Kirk, *The Vision of God* (1950), p. 61.

99

the world'. Yes, but this expression must be interpreted in the light of others in the Book of Common Prayer, where it is said that we are to renounce not the world as such but 'the vain pomp and glory of the world with all covetous desires of the same' (baptism service) or 'the pomps and vanities of this wicked world' (1928 confirmation service). That is to say, the world is here regarded as a system that is set up as a substitute for God, and to whose specious charms it is easy to become enslaved. What we are to renounce, as we are to renouce the devil and all his works, is what I call unholy worldliness.

What I am going to maintain is that our right relation to the world cannot be adequately covered by the formulas either of world-renunciation or of world-affirmation. Our right relation to the world is more involved than that: it can only be brought out dialectically, that is by saying Yes and No: indeed, by saying Yes and No and then Yes again. If I now proceed to say what I want to say in the form of a thesis, an antithesis and a synthesis, it is only because this suggests itself as a convenient framework and not because I have any further sense of indebtedness to Professor Hegel.

First, then, the *thesis* is that God made the world—both the world of nature and the world of culture. Of the world of nature it is said that he saw it was good: could it receive a stronger preliminary affirmation than that? The world of culture is from the outset of the Bible treated more ambiguously. God made man with his powers of creating culture and evidently intended those powers to be used and developed; but the fact that in the Genesis mythology the discovery of the various arts and technics is ascribed to the descendants of Cain may be taken as a sign of how readily they lend themselves to abuse and of how generally they have in fact been abused since the dawn of history. Still, the important point here is that according to the Old Testament mankind, and

God's chosen people in particular, are called to serve him in the life of this world and not merely to use this world as a dreary place of preparation for a life or world to come. 'The earth is the Lord's, and the fulness thereof', and we are meant so to regard it. Solomon in all his glory really was glorious—and is glorious. The men of the Old Testament would have protested as strongly as Mrs Margaret Knight did against a Christian contributor to *The Observer* who had written: 'It is not the fundamental concern of religion to bring order or civilisation to this world. Its fundamental concern is not with life but with death.'[1] Equally we may say the men of the Old Testament would have sympathized with Stewart Headlam when he said that a sermon by Dr Pusey to Cambridge under-graduates on the imminence of death was inexpressibly tedious. We must all have noticed how hard and how ingeni-ously Christian divines have to work in order to find in the Old Testament even premonitions of a life, worthy of the name, beyond the grave, and we know that the doctrine of resurrection was a late importation into Judaism.

Again, it is an awkward fact for Christian sectaries, and for those churchmen who now want to sever the traditional nexus between civil and ecclesiastical society, that in the Old Testa-ment not only is there no separation between Church and State but no clear line is drawn between what some call the 'religious' and the 'secular' orders. I say it *is* an awkward fact for the sectarian-minded: but perhaps I should say that they would find it awkward, were it not that they lightly skip over the testimony of the Old Testament and endeavour to found a norm for the relations between Church and society in the abnormalities of the New Testament.

I would suggest that the thesis of the Bible with regard to the life of this world—its primary and unsophisticated affirmation

[1] *The Observer*, June 3 and 24, 1956.

of the world—is exemplified in David whom we may take here as a paradigmatic figure. David in whom the physical and psychic vitalities are conspicuously present: David who was at once shepherd and psalmist and king: David who fought when it was necessary, with all his might, against powerful animals and powerful men; David who danced, with all his might, before the Ark of God: David the epic friend and the epic lover and the epic father (O Absalom, my son, my son): David the poet laureate and the beloved commander who would not drink of the water from the well of Bethlehem, for which he had longed, but poured it out unto the Lord: David who never lost his tenderness and *joie de vivre* though he had to cope with toughs like Joab: David whose soul 'was bound in the bundle of life' with the Lord his God and who was 'the man after God's own heart'.

So much at present for the thesis: now for the *antithesis*. Though the Old Testament is strikingly world-affirming, and exhibits God's interest, as well as man's, in everything to do with the life of the world, yet from the beginning it leaves us in no doubt that a dark shadow lies across the world. This world never has been the Paradise it might have been. Man's power to love, which is his most godlike capacity, with fatal ease degenerates into lust. His power to build, which represents his call to share in the work of the Creator, all too quickly produces towers of Babel. Cities and civic life with their splendid possibilities of culture and community often share, and deserve to share, the fate of Sodom and Gomorrah and of Babylon. The time came when the house of David itself, which began with such high promise, was found to be in ruins (see Amos 9.11). The fierce judgments of God upon the abuse by mankind, and by his chosen people in particular, of the sublime worldly powers and possibilities, which he had entrusted to them, was declared again and again by the mouth of his holy prophets that have been since the world began. And as we approach the horizon of the Old Testament these prophetic denunciations, which were however usually attended by promises of a better world and of a better worldliness beyond the impending doom, give way to the bizarre visions of apocalyptic in which the final dissolution of this world is predicted and portrayed.

The denunciation and the renunciation of the world culminates, however, not in an apocalyptist but in the return of Elijah —in John the Baptist. If David is the paradigmatic representative of the primary Yes that the Bible says to the world, John the Baptist is the paradigmatic representative of the No that must always be said in the next breath. You will see what I mean if I quote a passage from F. W. Robertson's sermon on 'The Word and the World':

> It was John's lot to be born into the world in a period of highly-advanced society; and in that hot-bed of life-fictions, Jerusalem, the ardent mind of the young man found nothing to satisfy the cravings of its desire. He wanted something deeper and truer than the existing systems could afford him. He went to the Sadducee and the Pharisee in vain. He found no life in the Jewish ritual—no assistance from the Rabbis. He went into the wilderness to commune with God, to try what was to be learned from Him by a soul in earnest, without church, ministers, or ordinances. The heavens spoke to him of purity, and the river by his side of God's eternity. Locusts and honey, his only food, taught him that man has a higher life to nourish than that which is sustained by epicurean luxuries. So disciplined John came back to his countrymen. As might be expected, no elaborate theology formed any part of his teaching. 'We want a simpler, purer, austerer life. Let men be real. Fruits worthy of repentance—fruits, fruits, not profession. A new life. Repent.' That was the burden of John's message.[1]

[1] *Sermons by F. W. Robertson*, Fourth Series, p. 148.

The austere figure of John the world-renouncer is for ever embedded hard by the centre of the gospel—hard by the Incarnate Lord himself. He is the essential Forerunner of the world's Redeemer and of the world's redemption. His message had not only once upon a time but it has always to prepare the way for the message of the Christ. I shall return to this point later.

But to come now to what for convenience I call the *synthesis*. When the Christ came, he accepted the baptism of John and gave a permanent endorsement to his mission and his message. But the Christ himself was not a world-renouncer after the Baptist's example. Where John came neither eating nor drinking, he came both eating and drinking and was charged with gluttony and winebibbing. The Christ came not wailing but piping so that not only that generation but all generations might dance. But we must not simplify matters here.

In the Christ and his Holy Spirit, who are one and whose work is one, the thesis, the antithesis and the synthesis are incarnate. First, there is his Yes to the worlds of nature and culture, to the physical and psychic and social vitalities. The very fact of his becoming flesh, and his birth into the world, constitute an ineffaceable signature, and the Gospels are the dictionary of the Christ's elemental and articulate affirmation of the world. I need only quote a few sentences from Hastings' *Dictionary of Christ and the Gospels*:

The beauty and charm of the visible world appealed to Him (Matt. 6.26, 28). Its incidents furnished illustrations for His sermons (Mark 4.3; Matt. 25.14). He participated in its festivals (John 2.1ff.), and contrasted Himself with one whose asceticism disparaged its good cheer (Matt. 11.18f.). Again, the claims of this world's lawful authorities always received His ready acknowledgement . . . (Mark 12.17; Matt. 17.27). Further in His thought the welfare of men is by no means a merely spiritual matter. . . . Christ calls His followers not to neglect the temporal world, much less to despise it, but to recognize that they have a function to fulfil in it by permeating every part of its life with beauty and truth (Matt. 5.13-16, 13.33; John 17.15).[1]

But to say no more than that would be like stopping short at the Galilean idyll. On any count, the Christ of the Gospels is not a simple world-affirmer. No doubt he identified himself with the world and its activities and consecrated its delights by participating in them. Indeed, he so identified himself with the original creation and so absorbed into himself the poisons by which it had been defaced, that he became the author and head of the new creation and of a restored world. As Father Thornton has said: 'In becoming "flesh" the Word made himself one with "all flesh", that is, with all creaturely life in this world of his creation. He who is in the bosom of the Father, he who himself holds this living cosmos in his embrace, having penetrated to its heart, became its offspring. . . . When the Creator thus entered into his creation and identified himself with it, he became its "Head" in a new sense.'[2]

He identified himself with a world that had become alienated from God, and in so doing reconciled it to God. In the words of Dietrich Bonhoeffer:

That God loved the world and reconciled it with himself in Christ is the central message proclaimed in the New Testament. It is assumed there that the world stands in need of reconciliation with God but that it is not capable of achieving it by itself. The acceptance of the world by God is a miracle of the divine compassion. . . .

In the body of Jesus Christ God took upon himself the sin of the whole world and bore it. There is no part of the world, be it never so forlorn and never so godless, which is not accepted by God and reconciled with God in Jesus

[1] D. C. G., ii. 840f.
[2] L. S. Thornton, The Dominion of Christ (1950), ii. 130.

Christ. Whoever sets eyes on the body of Jesus Christ in faith can never again speak of the world as though it were lost, as though it were separated from Christ; he can never again with clerical arrogance set himself apart from the world. The world belongs to Christ.[1]

This is the theological presupposition of what I call 'holy worldliness'. As Bonhoeffer says elsewhere: 'A life in genuine worldiness is possible only through the proclamation of Christ crucified.'[2] Through Christ's self-identification with the world in its forlornness and its dereliction, and through his having become its suffering servant, it has become endowed again with the limitless possibilities of the original creation—even at those points or in those areas where it still *looks* most forlorn. For this reason the mystical Body of Christ, the community of his Holy Spirit, the Church, rightly seeks to identify itself with the whole life of the world and to serve it—instead of standing aloof or apart. The true Church refuses to respond to the puritan or sectarian admonition to come out of the accursed city and be a community as separate as possible from the world.

Certainly, the Church in identifying itself with the world and serving it has needed and always will need puritan admonitions and the recurrent raising of John the Baptist from the dead, for in its identification with the world the Church is exposed to many temptations: the temptation to lord it over the world instead of to serve it—the temptation to confound the Yes of the synthesis with the Yes of the thesis and to avoid the disciplines and ordeals of the antithesis—the temptation to forget the difference between affirming the world for its own sake and affirming it because of the mystery of its reconciliation and restoration in the Christ—or, in a word, the temptation to become blind to the difference between holy and unholy worldliness.

[1] D. Bonhoeffer, *Ethics* (1955), pp. 70f.   [2] Ibid., p. 263.

Holy worldliness will be the outcome of a constantly renewed Yes and No and Yes again to the world. All three movements or emphases—thesis, antithesis, synthesis—have their part to play in Christian sanctification and in Christian education. Let me try to illustrate what I mean, both negatively and positively, with some gleanings from the literature of holy worldliness.

The education of children should begin with the thesis— with an elemental Yes to the world, not with prematurely imposing the antithesis upon their unready minds. They should learn to live in the atmosphere of the Old Testament before being introduced to the New. David should be their hero, before they are sent up to the Baptist and then to the Son of David who was David's Lord. Before they are chastened and humbled by the Law that condemns, they should be allowed to live the life of which St Paul said: 'I was once alive apart from the Law' (Rom. 7.9). Sanday and Headlam (*ad loc.*) point out that 'the frieze of the Parthenon is the consummate expression of a life that does not look beyond the morrow and and has no inward perplexities to trouble its enjoyment of today'. There is a striking passage in Emmanuel Mounier's *The Spoil of the Violent*, which illustrates how this elemental enjoyment of the world may be inhibited by a 'Christian upbringing':

Instead of being confronted from the very start with the whole sweep of the landscape of love, the young Christian is, eight times out of ten, first subjected to a powerful injection of 'moraline', and the first watchword of the moralist campaign is mistrust, caution: mistrust of the instincts and struggle against the passions. The first sentiment we inculcate in that being whom we are concerned to make into an example of moral health and a passionate lover of the infinite, is fear of the force which should serve as the root of his spiritual growth. . . . Whoever spends his youth

restraining, repressing and repelling, can respond to life
only with gestures of negation and withdrawal: initiative
and creativeness, like love, spring only from interior attitudes of generous openness. In all this we have the origin
of that dreary and somewhat stupid sadness that one often
sees on the faces of those entering and leaving churches and
chapels.[1]

By way of contrast, mark some words of Lady Violet Bonham
Carter describing her youth, which I would apply more widely
than she intended: 'Up went the curtain on the world. And
what a world! I loved it at first sight—and plunged into it head
foremost. There was no ice to break—the water was warm—
and I was swimming.'[2] That is how it should be to begin with,
and this is an experience that should periodically come to us
all afresh on the way to Christian sanctification. Anyhow, this
is the first wholesome initiation into a holy worldliness, and
blessed are those who are thus baptized into the world.

But, secondly, woe unto those who are never baptized into
anything else. Woe unto those who never go on to discover
and to face the strangeness of the world, the chill and the homelessness of its present condition, and who do not perceive its
power to seduce and degrade those who just take what it
offers and who never learn to say No to it.

Mind you, I am not joining in the chorus of ecclesiastics
which is always turning on a dirge about the materialism, the
paganism, the self-indulgence, of contemporary man. It is not
clear to me that it is on world-renunciation that contemporary
man falls down, or that lack of self-discipline is the cause of
his paleness. I should like to be more confident than I am that
contemporary man is affirming the world with zest and with
all his might. Geoffrey Gorer says that when he was going

[1] E. Mounier, *The Spoil of the Violent* (1955), pp. 39ff.
[2] *The Listener*, 28 June 1956.

through the answers to his questionary (which he calls a 'questionnaire'), in preparation for his book, *Exploring English Character*, he found himself constantly making the same notes: first, 'What dull lives most of these people appear to lead!' and, secondly, 'What good people!'[1] I suspect that there is plenty of world-renunciation in the conduct of modern man, though to his loss it is not interpreted as such. There is the extraordinary collective asceticism of our society—the clocking in, the commuting, the tax-paying, the heroic fortitude of the queues, the great discovery that *men* can and should and do wash up. Our pastors and spiritual directors might help us to relate all this to the paradigmatic figure of John the Baptist, instead of thinking up some fresh little bits of religiosity for us.

Whether or not there is a clue to anything there, we can lay it down that only those who have been brought to the Baptism of John can go on to receive the Baptism of the Spirit. Here again, F. W. Robertson says what I want to say:

It is a matter of no small importance that the baptism of John should precede the baptism of Christ; that is, a strict life, scrupulous regularity, abhorrence of evil—perhaps even something too austere, the usual accompaniment of sincerity at the outset—should go before the peace which comes of faith in Christ. First the blade, *then* the ear, then the full corn in the ear. You cannot have the harvest first. There is an order in the development of the soul as there is in the development of the year of nature, and it is not safe to *force*. Nearly two thousand years were spent in the Divine government in teaching the Jews the meaning of holiness, the separation of right from wrong. And such must be the order of the education of children and of men. The Baptism of Repentance before the Baptism of the Spirit.[2]

This Baptism of Repentance is not a thing that is received

---

[1] G. Gorer, *Exploring English Character* (1955), p. 303.
[2] Robertson, op. cit., p. 150.

once and for all and is then left behind. The Christian Year contains its own reminders that it has to be received again and again; though even at such times, lest we should become too unworldly, we are especially encouraged to sing *Benedicite, omnia opera* at morning prayer.

The Christian Year has indeed abundant reminders that what has been renounced is also given back. 'All things are yours', so the New Testament declares. But all things cannot now be just taken and enjoyed as they were to be at first. Holy worldliness is the working out in practice of a dialectical relation to the world and to all things that are therein. Emmanuel Mounier puts it thus:

> The duty of incarnation, if we were faithful to the meaning of the world, would oblige us to maintain simultaneously, at each moment of time, the most completely contradictory-to-good-sense positions; to die to the world, even while we committed ourselves to it; to deny the everyday, and to save it; to sorrow over our sins, and to rejoice in the new man; to reckon of value only what is inward, but to spread ourselves abroad throughout nature in order to conquer the whole of life for inwardness; to recognize in ourselves the dependence of a nothing and the liberty of a king. . . .[1]

Dietrich Bonhoeffer was, it seems so to me, saying much the same thing when he talked about 'religionless Christianity'. 'It is only', he said, 'by living completely in this world that one learns to believe. . . . This is what I mean by "worldliness"— taking life in one's stride, with all its duties and problems, its successes and failures, its experiences and helplessness. It is in such a life that we throw ourselves utterly in the arms of God and participate in his sufferings in the world and watch with Christ in Gethsemane. . . .'[2]

I should say that Mounier is describing holy worldliness

[1] *The Spoil of the Violent*, pp. 22f.

[2] D. Bonhoeffer, *Letters and Papers from Prison* (1953), p. 169.

when he speaks of 'a Christianity of the open air', and contrasts it with what the bourgeoisie have turned Christianity into.

The bourgeois house is a shuttered house, the bourgeois heart, a heart circumspect and cautious. The bourgeois would like to turn the catholic, apostolic Church into the back parlour of a shop, a confidential salon where anaemic virtues stagnated in a curtained half-light, ignorant of everything unconnected with ecclesiastical gossip, the troubles of a pious clique and the sterile confidences of lonely lives. The average devout catholic of one of our small towns carries his universe in his pocket. You must look elsewhere for the stage of the great elementary dramas of our time.[1]

A friend, with whom I had been recently discussing this subject, wrote to me afterwards as follows:

I believe that far too many of us resort to a *world-evading* type of religion through sheer cowardice. We cannot face either the tensions or the risks of trying to be in the world and not of it. So we busy ourselves with so-called religious activities—and become Holy Joes, pious women and what have you, devoting more and more time to 'religious' activities—including not only retreats but missions to win others to . . . the practice of the same escapist and pietistic habits. The vicious circle once formed it becomes harder and harder to break.

Unquestionably, there will be great risks in a Christianity of genuine worldliness: for it means living in the open air; it means living with men and serving them in all those areas where Christ is never named though they belong to him, or where he is named only to be misunderstood or reviled. Christians who carry their faith out there will need to be sustained by a secret discipline such as that of which Bonhoeffer speaks in his *Letters and Papers from Prison*, but above all they will need to be sustained by belief in the Holy Ghost and in the

[1] *The Spoil of the Violent*, p. 36.

working of the Holy Ghost in the whole world and in all flesh.

Therefore, I conclude with a profession of faith in the Holy Ghost which I take from F. D. Maurice's little-known book, *The Conflict of Good and Evil*:

> I believe in a Spirit who is at work on the inner life of human society, who is contending with all that makes it brutal or effeminate, slavish or anarchical. I believe in a Spirit who is not content with the semblances of civility and manliness, of freedom or order, who seeks to deliver us from whatever makes us ungracious to each other, cowardly in our resolutions and acts, from whatever leads us to crouch to any tyrant, or to set up any form of self-will in our own hearts. I believe in a Spirit who can never be satisfied till He awakens real energies: till those energies bring forth fruit in action. I believe in a Spirit who carries on continuously a conflict with the sloth and feebleness in me and in my fellow-creatures: who will give them and me no rest till He casts out from us the devils of sloth and feebleness.[1]

Such a faith in the working of the Holy Ghost in the world joins hands with the superb prayer with which *The Spoil of the Violent* ends:

> Then let the sail be bent to the main-mast, and let the ship of the Faith, issuing out from the harbour where it lies rotting at anchor, sail before the wind towards the furthest star, indifferent to the darkness around it.[2]

[1] F. D. Maurice, *The Conflict of Good and Evil* (1865), pp. 202f.
[2] Op. cit., p. 85.

VI

THE WELFARE STATE: A CHRISTIAN VIEW[1]

'THE Welfare State' is an expression which we all now use as a matter of course. We assume that we know what we mean by it, until someone asks exactly what we do mean by it. It is an expression that has come into use quite recently—within the last ten years, I suppose; but it does not follow that the thing it is intended to designate has come into existence equally recently. It might be a new name for something that existed previously. So far as I know, no one has yet tried to discover who first used the expression, and when, and why. Providence may be reserving that piece of research for some future graduate on the look-out for a topic for an academic thesis. Leaving that investigation aside, I begin by asking what are the distinguishing characteristics of what has come to be called 'The Welfare State'—that is, the characteristics that distinguish it from other kinds of State.

Every kind of State, every form of civil government, in some measure looks after the welfare of its citizens, if only by the provision of law and order. According to the *laissez faire* school, which was dominant in the earlier part of the nineteenth century, the function of government ought to be kept down to the minimum that was consistent with public security. The best possible government was the least possible government. Government should do no more than hold the ring so as to enable the free play of natural forces and of individual competition to produce a happy harmony. A symbol of the unobtrusiveness of government in the nineteenth century may be

[1] Reprinted from *Theology*, December 1952.

seen in Walter Bagehot's remark in 1867 that 'so well is our Government concealed that if you tell a cabman to drive to Downing Street he will most likely never have heard of it':[1] a remark which certainly could not be made of the taxi-driver today.

The transition from the *laissez faire* kind of State to what we have now was gradual and piecemeal, in the English manner; it was not the result of an ideological conversion or of a sudden revolution. It was the effect more of economic and political pressures than of disinterested social idealism, though both were at work. But the process was so haphazard that many Englishmen went on for a long time, as some do to this day, professing a simple faith in *laissez faire* without realizing how in practice they themselves take for granted a whole complex of institutions and services which are quite incompatible with the political faith they profess.

This was pointed out seventy years ago by Sidney Webb in a passage which illustrates the difficulty of determining when and where the Welfare State began. Webb was dealing with the case of the typical individualist who says, 'Self-help, sir, individual self-help, that's what has made our city what it is.'

> The individualist town councillor (Webb pointed out) will walk along the municipal pavement, lit by municipal light and cleansed by municipal brooms with municipal water, and seeing, by the municipal clock in the municipal market, that he is too early to meet his children coming from the municipal school, hard by the county lunatic asylum and the municipal hospital, will use the national telegraph system to tell them not to walk through the municipal park, but to come by the municipal tramway, to meet him in the muni-cipal reading-room, by the municipal museum, art-gallery, and library, where he intends to consult some of the national publications in order to prepare his next speech in the

[1] Quoted in E. E. Reynolds, *Ourselves and the Community* (1935), p. 249.

municipal town-hall in favour of the nationalization of canals and the increase of Government control over the railway system.[1]

That was written in the eighteen-eighties. The process of providing for the public welfare by State action and regulation, whether through central or local government, went steadily on. Notable developments were the first provision of old age pensions in 1908, the first National Health Insurance Act in 1911, the establishment of the Ministry of Health in 1919, unemployment insurance in 1920, and so on. *The Times* newspaper has spoken of the Welfare State as the creation of the Asquith government before the first world war. In 1929 Sir George Newman said that to build a healthy race had become one of the primary objects of government. So far as etymology goes, Britain might at that time have been described as a Welfare State. How then does what we have had since the second world war so differ from what we had previously as to justify the use of this new name?

The answer seems to be that in three respects the second world war led to developments in the State's provision for the welfare of its citizens which were so considerable in degree as almost to constitute a difference in kind and to warrant a new name. First, there was a tremendous increase in the amount of expenditure on the social services. Whereas in 1900 the total annual cost of the social services was £36 millions and in 1939 it was £450 millions, in 1949 it was £1,800 millions; or, to put it differently, the annual cost of the social services per head of the population was in 1900 £1, in 1939 £9 14s., and in 1949 £36 14s.[2] Secondly, the post-war reconstruction included an unprecedented attempt on the State's part to co-ordinate

[1] See Mark Abrams, *The Welfare State: its nature and some of its problems* (1951), p. 5.

[2] Abrams, op. cit., pp. 6f.

and unify, as well as to expand, services which had hitherto grown up in piecemeal fashion, so that the social services invited a single comprehensive name as they had not done before. Thirdly, the nation as a whole and both the political parties are now agreed, as was not the case before, that the State must be so organized as to secure certain basic standards of living and health and opportunity for every citizen. The Welfare State has become the object of a national mystique: and it would be an affectation any longer to pretend that the god to which we have erected an altar is unknown.

As for a formal definition, I accept that of Miss Penelope Hall in her most enlightening book, *The Social Services of Modern England* (p. 303):

> The distinguishing characteristic of the Welfare State is the assumption by the community, acting through the State, of the responsibility for providing the means whereby all its members can reach minimum standards of health, economic security and civilized living, and can share according to their capacity in its social and cultural heritage.

I confess that until I read Miss Hall's book I had not realized how comprehensive and complex is the range and variety of the provisions that are now made for the welfare of all citizens in this country and in particular for all kinds of misfortune and disability. By and large all that legislation can do has now been done: the machinery, the institutions, required to actualize the Welfare State so defined are there. If the provisions that have been made by legislation are not actually or fully in operation, that is owing to deficiency in the number or quality of personnel in the social services, or to the need for more time for legislation to take effect or bear fruit, or to economic obstacles consequent upon the international situation. Undoubtedly there is very much yet to be done if the purpose of existing legislation is to be achieved. 'Highfalutin' phrases about social medicine are all very well', said a school medical officer in 1948; 'we in Salford still have the school lavatories to attend to.'[1] But the framework, or structure of the Welfare State, is there and needs only to be filled in as well, of course, as to be modified in detail in the light of experience. It should therefore be possible to form at any rate a provisional opinion from a Christian point of view (or from any other for that matter) about the merits of the enterprise to which this country has committed itself, and also about its limitations and about the drawbacks or dangers which commonly attend even the best enterprises in this world.

Perhaps it should be said at the outset that no one ought to claim that the Welfare State is the final norm or standard of what a State should be according to the Law of God. By the State, in this context, I mean the body politic as organized for civil rule and government. God has not ordained any particular form of State as a permanent or universal pattern: he has left it to political philosophers to do that, and happily we are not tied to their prescriptions. The Bible exhibits for our contemplation, with more or less equal complacency and reservation, everything from the simplest forms of patriarchal and tribal government to the vast cosmopolitan structure of the Roman Empire. The form or structure of a State is to be judged not by any abstract norm or doctrinaire ideal, but by whether in practice it provides a human society first with what is necessary for its existence and then with what is conducive to its wellbeing.

The maintenance of internal order and defence against external enemies are necessary for the existence of every society and therefore they are a universal function of every kind of civil government. Beyond that, it is the testimony of the law and the prophets in the Bible that a national community ought

[1] See Hall, op. cit., pp. 303f.

so to order its common life that the rapacity of the powerful is curbed and that the human needs of all its members, and indeed of the strangers within the gates, are met. But the extent to which these needs can be met depends naturally upon the resources that are available to this nation or that; and the manner in which they can best be met—whether by direct action or regulation on the part of the civil government or otherwise—varies according to the size, complexity, economic development, and traditional habits of any given State.

I shall return to this point in a moment from a rather different angle. For another way of reaching a Christian point of view on the Welfare State is to reflect upon the divine command 'Thou shalt love thy neighbour as thyself', and upon Christ's answer to the question 'Who is my neighbour?', and further upon the issue of Christ's work and the gift of his Spirit—namely, the creation of a new kind of community in which men of all classes and races are bound together by grace in a relationship of mutual love which is open to limitless expansion.[1] This new creation, of which only the first instalments are apparent yet, contains the promise that mankind is to become—in the end, at the last Day—a universal family, and can now be moving in that direction. There will be, there is already, a community in which like the limbs of a body all the members share a common life. It is such a common life— in Christ—which is the destiny that God has prepared for mankind.

[1] In an article on 'Problème et mystère du progrès humain' in the September-October 1952 number of *Nouvelle Revue Théologique*, Père E. Rideau, S.J., writes: 'Ouverte par la Résurrection du Christ, l'ère chrétienne est caracterisée par l'espérance . . . par l'*ouverture* de l'avenir, la possibilité de jaillissements, de surgissements et de reprises. Rien n'est absolument définitif et clos, les cercles où la conscience individuelle et collective voudrait s'enfermer sont fragiles et se brisent: l'esprit de renouvellement et d'invention travaille, en toute domaine, l'humanité. La grâce n'est qu'un autre nom de cette espérance lorsqu'elle manifeste plus visiblement la présence active de l'Esprit de charité.'

No earthly state is qualified to realize fully a common life of that kind: the Church itself realizes it only in an exceedingly ambiguous way—'as having nothing and yet possessing everything'. At the same time the common life in the body of Christ, now that it has emerged in history, has become a norm or standard by which every human society, ecclesiastical or civil, must be tested and to which it should seek to approximate in whatever ways and to whatever degree it can. In some respects every state will always contradict society as re-created by Christ, and must belong to the old world and not to the new—for example, by its use of coercion. On the other hand, those elements of the common life which belong to the sphere of the state are not impervious to the new creation, and the state may be the means by which men may realize here and now some genuine approximation to membership one of another in the body of Christ. But the form which such approximation can best take depends on the size, complexity, and economic development and traditional habits of each particular state.

If then it should be the case that, in our historic circumstances, the 'Welfare State' is the best means by which the human needs of all citizens can be met—by which as a national community we can be assisted to love our neighbours as ourselves (justice is love operating at a distance)—and by which we can best approximate to certain elements of the common life in the body of Christ, then we could say that the Welfare State—however, and from whatever motives, it has come into existence—in accordance with both the law of God and the gospel of Christ.

There is still the question whether the Welfare State really is the best or most effective means by which these aims can be realized in our historic circumstances. The justification of the Welfare State in this connexion becomes apparent when we contrast 'an agricultural society made up of close-knit and almost self-contained family groups living in isolated communities, each responsible for the care of its own poor and unfortunate', and 'a highly industrialized urban society'[1] such as we have now. In the former case the provision by a central government of a complex of social services would have been impracticable and superfluous. The care of the needy and unfortunate could satisfactorily be left, not indeed to the operation of natural forces, but to the traditional *mores* which bound the members of families and local communities to one another in mutual care, loyalty, and responsibility. And in Christendom there was in addition in most localities a monastery or similar institution which provided for those who were not cared for by their own family.

In a highly industrialized age, on the other hand, the family is no longer self-contained or self-dependent; and resources are available which make possible a more adequate and a more equal provision for human needs throughout a whole nation with its many millions of population. Further, in this kind of society we are all physically interdependent as we were not before, and this fact requires that we should recognize and make effective a corresponding degree of moral interdependency. It seems inevitable that in this kind of society—with its mobility, cosmopolitanism, and its tendency to deracination—traditional *mores* and the constraint of custom lose much of their authority and power. They need, to say the least, to be complemented by the constraint of legislation, and by the provision of machinery and institutions which will enable—and if necessary compel—men to care for one another, as well as for themselves, to an extent and on a scale that was impossible under the older conditions. Thus President Truman was justified in saying that the opponents of a national health

[1] Hall, op. cit., p. 4.

service in the U.S.A. 'wanted to go back to the horse and buggy days'.[1]

Therefore I conclude that Christians ought to welcome and approve the general idea of the Welfare State. But, when that has been said, there are, in the first place, still a good many open questions about how the general idea can best be worked out from where we are at present and how its provisions can be both improved and safeguarded from abuse. And, in the second place, while we may agree that the Welfare State is a good thing, it is not everything, and it may get in the way of other good things, so that a Christian will accompany his Yes with a No. If it is important to see why we should say Yes to the Welfare State, it is also important to see where and how we should say No.

Before enlarging a little on those points I would interject that there are two enormous questions which I say nothing about in this essay because, if I broached them at all, I should become involved in inquiries and speculations which would carry me far beyond my present subject. I mean the questions, first, whether on a long view it is going to be possible to provide the population of the world, and of this country in particular, with sufficient food, let alone with other amenities; secondly, whether this country is justified in keeping its own standard of living as high as possible irrespective of the standards of living in other parts of the British Commonwealth or of the world.

Leaving those questions aside as beyond the scope of this essay, I come now, first, to what are open questions in the working out of the Welfare State. Some of these are no doubt purely technical, but others are certainly, from a Christian point of view, frontier questions. It is questions of this kind that ought to be engaging the thought and action of Christians.

[1] See *The Times* newspaper, 17 September 1952.

I will mention a few examples. How far does the viability of the Welfare State depend on there being in citizens generally a much higher degree of consciousness about the nature and aims of society and a keener sense of responsibility for the well-being of the whole community than there have been in the past? This is parallel to the question Mr Middleton Murry often raises[1] about whether our sort of democracy, if it is to work, does not demand a new kind of political consciousness in its citizens. If so, how is it to be evoked? Then there is the question, what are the new tasks that are proper to each of the political parties now that the Welfare State is an accepted fact?[2] Again, the Welfare State by definition is concerned not only to secure physical efficiency but to meet human needs.[3] There is obviously a good deal of room for debate about what human needs are, and which of them are susceptible to the kind of provision the Welfare State can make: this is a question that is especially acute in the sphere of education. Again, several of the social services are handicapped by a shortage of suitably qualified staff.[4] Since what the Welfare State will turn into depends largely on the quality and calibre of the persons who operate its services, the question of their recruitment and training should be a matter of great concern, not least to Christians. And since many of the functions which used to be performed by ordained ministers of the churches will in future be performed by the officers of the Welfare State, the churches

[1] E.g. in *The Free Society*, pp. 145f.

[2] See 'Some Neglected Aspects of the Welfare State' by Daniel Jenkins in *The Frontier* (October 1952), pp. 387-400.

[3] The word 'welfare', says Viscount Samuel, speaking of the Welfare State, must include not only 'material comfort' but also 'knowledge, and virtue, and personal liberty and self-respect' (*The Spectator*, 12 September 1952).

[4] For example, social case workers (Hall, p. 118), children's homes (ibid., p. 200), the youth employment service (ibid., p. 206), and youth leaders (ibid., p. 231).

might be showing more enterprise than they are yet in offering training in a lay theology and in a relevant spiritual discipline for all these new pastors of the Lord's people.

There are also open and important questions about what can best be done by central government and what by local government, and again about what can still best be done by voluntary societies, in which of course Christian interests are closely involved. Voluntary societies, it need hardly be said, do not mean societies of volunteers. Just as the state services depend upon some people doing voluntary work under their auspices, so the voluntary societies may employ salaried professional workers. A voluntary society is defined by the fact that it owes its existence to the initiative and continued support of individuals and groups, and not to the state, but there is no reason why the state should not grant it financial help. It is not difficult to see that there should always be scope for voluntary social work, since this is more free to pioneer with new experiments and to make mistakes, and so perhaps prepare the way for state action. On the other hand, there are some things, like marriage guidance and citizens' advice, that will always be better done by voluntary societies than by direct state action. It is less easy to see how voluntary societies are to survive under present conditions, and some city or town in England might well experiment with something on the lines of the 'Community Chests' which are now found in nearly all important centres in the U.S.A. and Canada.[1] More comprehensively, we can say that Christians should be watching, and contributing to, the working out of the Welfare State at every point with certain criteria in mind which do not come easily to all planners. I mean, is this or that provision or method calculated to nourish or cramp personal freedom and responsibility? Will it strengthen or weaken the family as a social

[1] See Hall, op. cit., pp. 292f.

institution? Some people are ready to give generalized answers based on partial experience or even on partial impressions, to questions about how the Welfare State is working out in these respects. None of the answers will be very convincing till a great deal more scientific field-work has been done, in the attempt to find out what are the actual results of the various social services in their effects on personal character and on family life.

Lastly, I said that there are likely to be more general Noes or notes of warning about the Welfare State which Christians may be moved to sound.

However positive our support of the Welfare State, if we thought that the British people were becoming exclusively preoccupied with material security and comfort, if we thought that our national idol was coming to be the idea of a planned society in which everyone will be comfortably off and have to work only moderately hard, in which morals will be easy-going and we shall be tolerant of one another's weaknesses—if we thought that, well then, we should have to declare in season and out of season that, while men must have bread to live, they cannot live by bread alone. That, of course, needs to be said, to myself most of all, but it is less clear to me than it is to many Christians that this ought to be the constant theme of our broadcasts to the British people.

Instead of denouncing the materialism of the age, which is a very easy thing to do, Christians would be better occupied in discovering how the evident tendency of the Welfare State to make us all preoccupied with security and cosiness can be effectively balanced by contrary provisions that will keep us aware of our ultimate insecurity except in the hands of our Saviour, and that will prevent our being cushioned against everything in the real world that makes for doubt, tension, struggle, loneliness, eccentricity, and dying to live. There is no need now for churches to agitate—as they should have done in the nineteenth century—for the introduction of elementary social justice, nor need they any longer seek to compete with the social services on their own ground. Churches should rather be now finding out how within the Welfare State they may become disturbing community centres where things are not made easy but are seen to be difficult, and where the dark and bewildering, as well as the glorious and reassuring, mysteries of existence, of which the Bible is the text-book, are revealed to the imagination of a famished generation.

This means that the Church has a long way to go from where it is at present: not that we need more attacks on utopianism, but we do need many more focal points to which all in whom there are the rudiments of the divine discontents are tempted to gravitate. It means that there will be a more disturbing, haunting quality and power than there is as yet in the visual arts and poetry and music to which the Church seems to be most commonly wedded. It means that the last thing people who go to church will be inclined to say is that it was a very nice service.

VII

BISHOP GORE AND LIBERAL
CATHOLICISM[1]

SINCE the last Gore Memorial Lecture was delivered
we have had to lament the death of Dr Prestige,
Gore's biographer. All who have read that biography
must feel permanently indebted to its author, and it
is to be hoped that it will introduce many future generations of
readers to one who was a great Christian and a great churchman. I will confess that, at the time of its publication, I wished,
and I wish still more now, that Bishop Gore had been allowed
a proper, two- or three-decker, biography. It might not have
been so widely read in these thin days, but it would have been
a source-book of immense value to historians.

As during recent months I have been thinking about Bishop
Gore and re-reading his works, I have repeatedly felt the force
of these words which Dr N. P. Williams wrote not long after
Gore's death: 'The true mental and moral stature of this
remarkable man could hardly be appreciated during his life-
time; but his figure grows greater in retrospect as we recede
from it.'[2] Certainly he made an unforgettable impression on
all those of us who were brought into contact with him. One
of his friends described him as a 'truly "numinous" figure'.[3]
Bishop Hensley Henson said that Gore had 'that strange con-
quering quality which is sometimes called genius'.[4] The only
person who inspired me as a young man with a greater sense
of awe was Frank Weston, Bishop of Zanzibar.

[1] The Gore Memorial Lecture delivered in Westminster Abbey on
17 November 1955.

[2] N. P. Williams in *Northern Catholicism* (1933), p. 144.

[3] J. Conway Davies in *Theology*, November 1932, p. 259.

[4] *Retrospect of an Unimportant Life*, i. 208.

In this lecture, however, my intention is to speak not so much about Gore's character as about what he stood for—his theological position. In one of his Gore Lectures Dr Prestige said that 'Gore claimed and loved the name of "Liberal Catholic" asserting his spiritual kinship with men like Döllinger and Lord Acton', but Dr Prestige went on to say that 'since the title "Liberal" is used in different senses and gives rise to misunderstanding, it is perhaps better to describe Gore as a Christian rationalist'.[1] That may or may not be so, but before we give up calling Gore a Liberal Catholic, it may be worth while to inquire why that is what he liked to be called, and what he meant by Liberal Catholicism. Anyhow that is what I am going to attempt to do in this lecture.

Make no mistake about it; Gore was very closely attached to the term Liberal Catholicism and to what he meant by it. He was prepared to stand for it, alone, if necessary. During the controversy about Hensley Henson's appointment to the see of Hereford, Gore wrote to an old friend: 'I remain embracing with all my conviction an ideal of Liberal Catholicism which, it appears, no one is willing to listen to, neither "Catholics" nor "Liberals" nor the man in the street, nor anybody else except a very few old ladies and gentlemen. I suppose God has other purposes for the world and the Church.'[2] That was written at a moment of acute depression. Usually he spoke more confidently and more hopefully, though never complacently. 'The world's need of a liberal catholicism will surely become increasingly apparent,' he declared in 1909.[3] 'A really liberal catholicism . . . is the world's best hope for religious unity.'[4] He saw in the Church of England, despite all that irked him, an embodiment of that hope. 'I have always

---

[1] G. L. Prestige, *The Soul of a Prophet* (1948), p. 14.
[2] Prestige, *Life of Charles Gore* (1935), p. 407.
[3] *Orders and Unity*, p. 205.   [4] Ibid., p. 199.

claimed', he said, 'that we in the Church of England represent a liberal catholicism.'[1] And again: 'If the Anglican Church has a real message and vocation, it is because it embodies [the] principles of a liberal or comprehensive Catholicism.[2] He spoke of 'the position which God has given to us Anglicans to maintain—the position which is best described as a liberal catholicism'.[3]

Before asking what Gore meant by Liberal Catholicism, I propose to spend a few minutes considering what the expression had meant before Gore adopted it. He himself said that 'Liberal Catholicism is a name which has a great history and represents a great idea'.[4] In saying that, he must have had in mind those groups and movements in the Roman Church which had borne the name 'Liberal Catholic'. So far as I know, the name had not previously been applied to any Anglicans though, if anyone had thought of it, it might suitably have been applied to such pre-*Lux Mundi* Anglicans as F. D. Maurice,[5] Dean Church,[6] Mr Gladstone, and J. H. Shorthouse.[7]

In the Roman Church the first so-called Liberal Catholics were Lamennais[8] and those associated with him in the episode

[1] *The Basis of Anglican Fellowship*, pp. 4, 23.

[2] *Oxford Diocesan Magazine*, 1915; see Prestige, *Life*, p. 378.

[3] *Orders and Unity*, p. iv.   [4] See Prestige, *Life*, p. 97.

[5] Cp. C. F. G. Masterman, *Frederick Denison Maurice* (1907), p. 221.

[6] Dr Prestige actually describes Dean Church as 'the veteran leader of English Liberal Catholicism'. *Life of Gore*, p. 84.

[7] Cp. W. L. Knox and A. R. Vidler, *The Development of Modern Catholicism* (1933).

[8] Hensley Henson, referring to *Lux Mundi*, said that Gore 'would play in the Church of England a part similar to that which, earlier in the century, Lamennais had played *mutatis mutandis* in the Church of France' (*Retrospect*, i. 155); but I am not aware of any evidence that Gore was influenced by Lamennais, unless it be that in 1896 he was corresponding with Wilfrid Ward about Lamennais and that as late as 1923 he was reading *Parles d'un Croyant* during a visit to Prague (see Prestige, *Life*, pp. 173, 470).

of the *Avenir*.[1] Their professed aim was both to liberalize catholicism and to catholicize liberalism. While Lamennais had an immense, all-round vision of a renovation of the Roman Church to meet the needs and conditions of a changed world (a vision, the far-sightedness of which many Roman Catholics today acknowledge), yet the particular reason why his enterprise was called 'Liberal Catholic' was that he advocated the abandonment by the Church of its privileged position in the state and its espousal of the cause of equal freedom for all religious bodies. The Church should in future separate itself from civil governments and depend only on the spiritual authority of the papacy. This first Catholic welcome to the policy of 'a free Church in a free state' was quickly nipped in the bud because of its ultramontanism as well as because of its liberalism.

In the subsequent phases of the Liberal Catholic movement[2] the liberal and the ultramontane elements diverged and indeed became bitterly hostile to one another. Montalembert and Falloux had no more violent opponent than Louis Veuillot. Liberal Catholicism in France continued to have primarily a political character, as for example in the campaign for educational liberty, though later in the case of Dupanloup, Gratry and others it broadened out and stood for meeting the modern mind so far as possible, or at least for not offending its axioms more than was necessary. On the other hand, as Wilfrid Ward says, 'Louis Veuillot and his friends held the Church as a besieged city against the modern world . . . they entrenched themselves behind scholastic bulwarks, and looked askance at the complex modern movement, which was at once

[1] See my book, *Prophecy and Papacy: a study of Lamennais, the Church and the Revolution* (1954).

[2] See Wilfrid Ward, *W. G. Ward and the Catholic Revival*, Chapter v; A. R. Vidler, *The Modernist Movement in the Roman Church*, Chapters iii-vi.

anti-Christian, political, and scientific . . . suspecting the
modern "liberties" and longing for the day to return when
the Church had excluded the very breath of error and
doubt.'[1]

In Germany Liberal Catholicism was intellectual rather than
political. The Munich school, of which Dr Döllinger was the
chief light, urged the necessity of scientific freedom and historical criticism and the reconsideration of theological opinions
which new knowledge called in question. It was this element
that spread to England through Acton, and had a brief but
brilliant outburst in the *Rambler* and the *Home and Foreign
Review*.[2]

These Liberal Catholic groups or tendencies in the Roman
Church were suppressed or silenced in 1864 by the papal
encyclical *Quanta cura* and the Syllabus, and it was widely supposed that they had been finally rendered impossible by the
Vatican Council in 1870. But after the accession of Leo XIII
they began to reappear, and by the last decade of the century
were showing much liveliness, not least in England. On 18
August 1900 an anonymous Roman Catholic writer contributed an article entitled 'The Roman Catholic Broad Church'
to the Anglican journal, *The Pilot*, over whose directors Gore
presided. Here it was boldly asserted that 'the Vatican Council
was believed by many to have given the death-blow to Liberal
Catholicism. But . . . Liberal Catholicism is neither dead nor
dying.' If it was still alive, it was not the fault of the ecclesiastical authorities. A few months later (on 29 December 1900)
the English Roman Catholic Bishops issued a joint pastoral on
'Liberal Catholicism', which was afterwards endorsed by the
pope—a pronouncement that would be worth studying as a

[1] W. Ward, *Life of Newman*, i. 470.

[2] See W. Ward, *W. G. Ward and the Catholic Revival*, Chapter vi.

notable specimen of Illiberal Catholicism.[1] But I have said as much as is necessary, in the present context, about Liberal Catholicism in the Roman Church. I am not aware of any precise evidence about ways in which Gore was actually influenced by Döllinger, Acton or other Liberal Roman Catholics.

Before we come to grips with the question what Gore himself meant by Liberal Catholicism, it may be well to reflect a little on the variety of meanings that this term can have. The subject is complicated of course by the extraordinary multiguity of the words 'Liberal' and 'Liberalism'. When considering in what sense, if any, Newman was a Liberal Catholic, Professor Charles Saroléa wrote in 1908—and the case could be put even more strongly now: 'There does not exist in the vocabulary of politics or philosophy one single word which is more constantly misused and misunderstood than the word "liberalism". There exists every variety and type of liberal from the "free-thinker" who worships liberty as an idol, to the philosophical liberal who sees in liberty the condition of

[1] 'Some there were whose pride chafed under the restrictions imposed by religion. Not content with the vast fields of profane science and speculation open to them, and with the civil government of the world, which was theirs, they itched to have their hand in the government of the Church and in her teaching; or, if this could not be, they vainly strove to enforce their views by appeals to the Press and to public opinion. They conceived the idea . . . that the government of the Church should be largely shared by the laity as a right; that it was permissible for the faithful to correct abuses and scandals by recourse to the people and to the powers of the world rather than to the authorities of the Church. An obligation rested upon every one to think as the Church thought and to obey her voice, and not only where the subject-matter was one of Divine revelation or connected therewith but also wherever the subject-matter of the Church's teaching fell within the range of her authority; and that range comprised all that was necessary for feeding, teaching, and governing the flock. The "liberal Catholic" flattered himself that his own opinions were the outcome of a strong-minded, impartial, and philosophical spirit. . . . Indiscriminate reading was perhaps the most insidious form under which the poison of rationalism and unbelief was injected into the soul. . . .' See *The Times* newspaper, 29 December 1900.

intellectual and moral discipline, down to the conservative liberal who accepts liberalism as a necessary evil. The exact meaning of the word "liberal" must therefore be strictly defined by the circumstances of time and place and by the personal characteristics of the thinker whose conception of the term we attempt to describe.'[1]

That is wise advice, even if we confine our attention (as we must do here) to the epithet 'Liberal' when used in conjunction with 'Catholic' or 'Catholicism'. But we may usefully generalize to this extent: The epithet 'Liberal' when applied to a Catholic may have (i) a political, (ii) an ecclesiastical, (iii) a theological, or (iv) a personal connotation. (i) *First*, it may signify that such and such a Catholic is in favour of constitutional political liberties, and in particular that he is *not* set upon maintaining or reviving the medieval and post-Reformation union or alliance between church and state, but is in favour of their separation and of the equal treatment of all religions by the state. That is to say, a Liberal Catholic in this first sense of the term is one who wants liberty *for* the church and is prepared to pay the just price. (ii) In the *second* sense, a Liberal Catholic is one who wants liberty *in* the church. He is against —I do not say authority, but—authoritarianism in ecclesiastical government. He holds—whether or not he agrees with them— that there should be freedom in the church for the advocacy of new ideas and proposals for reform, and that they should be open for discussion by the laity as well as by the clergy. This type of Liberal Catholic would say that the only agreement worth having in a church is that of men who possess the right to differ, and he would subscribe to Archbishop Frederick Temple's dictum: 'If the conclusions are prescribed, the study is precluded.'

(iii) The *third* type of Liberal Catholic is one who, in regard

[1] C. Saroléa, *Cardinal Newman*, pp. 138f.

to matters of faith or order, holds and expresses opinions which depart from those that are traditional or at present generally received in the church, or at least he publicly commits himself to a more flexible interpretation of traditional formularies and ecclesiastical regulations than has hitherto been customary. This type of Liberal Catholic not only wants the church to provide freedom for reformers, but he is a reformer himself. (iv) When one speaks about a Liberal Catholic in the *fourth* sense, one is not necessarily saying anything at all about his opinions concerning civil or ecclesiastical polity. In this case the epithet 'liberal' (which should be spelt with a small initial letter) refers not to the man's opinions, but to the way he holds them. It refers to a certain kind of intellectual disposition or psychological temperament. Thus, if we call a man a liberal Catholic in this sense, we mean that there is nothing fanatical about him. He is not easily shocked. He is alive to the tendencies of his time. He is capable of discussing all questions dispassionately, and enjoys treating them as open, or at least as if they were open, though we may know very well that there is no likelihood of his changing his mind. A man can be a liberal Catholic in this sense without being one in any of the other senses. You might even come across a liberal Catholic in this sense who was a pillar of the strictest traditional orthodoxy, though I grant that the experience would be an unusual one. In any case, I hope it is clear that, in this and indeed in all senses, the opposite of Liberal Catholicism is not Orthodox Catholicism—to say that would be to prejudge all the issues— but Illiberal or Intransigent Catholicism.

The discrimination I have just made between four types of Liberal Catholic or of Liberal Catholicism will prove serviceable when we consider the nature of the Liberal Catholicism that Bishop Gore professed and practised. Evidently, when you hear *anyone* described as a Liberal Catholic, it is necessary to ask in what sense or senses he is being so described.

In the case of Bishop Gore, or of any other Anglican who claimed to be a Liberal Catholic, we have to ask not only what he meant by Liberal, but what he meant by Catholicism. When Roman Catholics speak of Catholicism, we know that they mean Roman Catholicism. I will however interject my satisfaction that Pope Pius XII recently took exception to the use of the term 'Catholicism' as a definition of his Church.[1] His objection would have pleased F. D. Maurice who held that a Catholic *system* was 'one of the greatest enemies of the Catholic *Church*',[2] and who rejoiced that in the liturgy he had a protection against every kind of 'ism.[3] I think Gore would have appreciated this objection to the term 'Catholicism' if it had been pointed out to him, but the objection does not seem to have occurred to him and he freely used the term without any apparent scruple. Therefore on this occasion I shall do so too.

One might say, of course, that the whole corpus of Gore's published work was an exposition of what Catholicism meant to him and of what he meant by Catholicism. His most concise definition, so far as I recall, is to be found in the first chapter of his book *Catholicism and Roman Catholicism*, published in 1923. There he says: 'I mean by Catholicism what is generally meant by the term in histories of early Christianity, viz. that way of regarding Christianity which would see in it not merely or primarily a doctrine of salvation to be apprehended by individuals, but the establishment of a visible society

---

[1] 'The Church does not act only as an ideological system. She is doubtless defined as such when the term 'Catholicism' is used, for this term is neither customary nor fully adequate for her. She is much more than a simple ideological system: she is a reality just as visible as nature, as a people or a State, are realities. She is an organism.' Papal Allocution to the Tenth Congress of Historical Sciences. See *The Tablet*, 24 September 1955.

[2] See *Life of F. D. Maurice*, i. 308.   [3] Ibid., i. 512.

as the one divinely constituted home of the great salvation, held together not only by the inward Spirit but also by certain manifest and external institutions.'[1]

Gore started from the position that the Catholic Church was the Old Israel of God, reorganized by Christ. 'When we say "I believe in one holy catholic and apostolic church" we mean that we believe a visible society, however full of human infirmity, is yet the special organ of the Holy Spirit and of the living Christ in the world.'[2] Because the New Israel is 'free and open to all the world', it is 'by its very nature destitute of those links which bind nations and most human fellowships together, such as a common country or language or racial tradition or common occupation'. Instead, it was 'provided from the beginning with special links to preserve its continuity and cohesion—especially three: (1) The authority of an apostolic ministry which perpetuated itself in various grades. . . . (2) Certain sacraments of fellowship in which all were bound to participate. . . . (3) The common teaching or rule of faith or tradition, which was to be accepted by all the members of the Church as the word of God.'[3]

It was Gore's way to draw out what he meant by Catholicism by contrasting it with Protestantism, on the one hand, and with *Roman* Catholicism, on the other. Take first the contrast with Protestantism. Here it should be borne in mind that Gore's period was the period of the popularity, not to say the ascendancy, in the Protestant world of what perhaps may not unfairly be called those reduced versions of Christianity associated with the names of Adolf Harnack in Germany and of R. J. Campbell and the New Theology in England. In 1914 Gore spoke of 'the amazingly rapid disintegration of the distinctive

[1] Op. cit., p. 1. See also *The Holy Spirit and the Church*, Chap. ix, for an outline of what Gore regarded as the essential content of the Catholic faith.

[2] *The Holy Spirit and the Church*, p. 300.   [3] Ibid., p. 283.

creeds of Protestantism',[1] which is not exactly what any knowledgeable observer would say today. Gore was in many ways a prophet, but he did not foresee the remarkable change that would come over Protestant theology and Protestant churchmanship during the quarter of a century after his death.[2] The popular Protestantism that he saw around him, especially in England and America, struck him as 'a cheap philanthropic gospel unaccompanied by any careful or exacting doctrine about God and sin and redemption'.[3] It made light of the whole idea of the Church. It was fundamentally individualistic. With it he constantly contrasted 'Catholicism or the sacramental method in religion' which however (he said) was 'in no way opposed to all that can legitimately be called Evangelical'.[4]

On the other hand, Gore constantly contrasted Catholicism with Roman Catholicism on the ground that that was a one-sided distortion of Catholicism. 'The Roman development of Christianity', he said, 'is a one-sided development: because it exaggerates and intensifies, with a strange disregard of ancient and catholic restraints, the principle of centralized government and sacerdotal authority and dogma.'[5] And again: 'The religion of the Roman Catholic Church presents all the appearance of a one-sided development of catholicity in the direction of autocracy. . . . The true development of the Church does not lie in the heightening and extension of the dogmatic claim by a logical process, which more and more tends to make the

[1] *The Basis of Anglican Fellowship*, p. 6.

[2] 'We see . . . the breaking down and weakening of the positive and distinctive types of Protestantism. The progress of this weakening is most marked. What force in Europe to-day is dogmatic Lutheranism, or the definite religion of Calvinism? How rapidly the distinctiveness of Baptist or Congregationalist or Methodist is merging in the common undenominational type of religion!' *Orders and Unity*, pp. 190f.

[3] Ibid., p. 24.   [4] *The Anglo-Catholic Movement Today*, p. 14.

[5] *Orders and Unity*, p. 196.

burden upon the intellect intolerable and swamps the freedom of the spirit; it lies rather in the constant self-adaptation of the Church to new demands of new races, new knowledge, new conditions of society.'[1] It was, Gore declared, for the Anglican Church, despite its many and grave shortcomings, 'to present a type of Catholicism which the world had forgotten, which should have priests but not be priest-ridden, and should accept the Catholic tradition but keep it purged by the free use of reason and an all-pervading scripturalness'.[2] But I have already begun to describe what Gore meant by a *Liberal* Catholicism.

Gore, who was more responsible than anyone for giving the nineteenth-century Catholic revival in the Church of England a new and liberal orientation, did not fail to explain that the Liberalism he favoured was something quite different from the utilitarian Liberalism to which the original Tractarians had been opposed.[3] In his book, *The Anglo-Catholic Movement Today*, (1925), he said that there were 'three modifications or enlargements of the original spirit and temper of the Anglo-Catholic Movement' which, in his judgment, it was necessary to welcome. These were, first, the acceptance of the principle of biblical criticism; secondly, the acceptance of the principle of social justice as a central and essential element of the Christian gospel; and thirdly, a more hopeful, or at least agnostic, attitude to the eternal destiny of people outside the Church.[4]

[1] *The Holy Spirit and the Church*, p. 343.   [2] Ibid., p. 353.

[3] See *The Anglo-Catholic Movement Today*, pp. 4, 17. The Liberalism which Newman and the Tractarians fought was, as Dean Church said, that form of modern thought that tended to destroy the basis of revealed religion, and ultimately of all that can be called religion at all. See his *Occasional Papers*, ii. 386. 'What Newman named "Liberalism",' said A. M. Fairbairn, 'was a single force disguised in many forms, rationalism in religion, revolution or reform in politics, Erastianism and latitudinarianism in church. It was the spirit of change, negation, disintegration, destruction.' *Catholicism Roman and Anglican*, p. 307. It was the task of Gore to discriminate between what was tolerable and desirable in all these tendencies and what was not.

[4] See op. cit., p. 24.

But those three points give only a limited idea of what Gore meant by Liberal Catholicism. I propose to fill in the picture by considering to what extent he was a Liberal Catholic in the four different senses I distinguished just now.

I begin then by asking to what extent Gore was a Liberal Catholic in the political sense. In particular did he favour the alliance or the separation of church and state? He was, as is well-known, in regard to English party politics, a Liberal—or a Radical with socialistic leanings.[1] With respect to the nexus between church and state, I note that on 5 November 1886 Hensley Henson made this entry in his journal: 'I went to the Puseyum and saw Gore. Had a talk with Stuckey Coles about Disestablishment. On the basis of his parochial experience he advocates Disestablishment. The main charge which he brings against the "Establishment" is the lack of discipline which it involves. Gore is in an absolute fix on the subject, pulled both ways, unable to make up his mind, waits the smash in indolent agony.'[2]

Gore paralysed by indecision—this was to be a very rare spectacle indeed. Long before the days of the Life and Liberty Movement, he was an ardent advocate of self-government for the Church,[3] and as time went on he came out more and more strongly in favour of Disestablishment. Thus in 1914: 'I think that Disestablishment, more than anything else, would throw us upon our principles. I doubt whether anything else will do so effectively.'[4] And ten years later: 'I believe the existence of an Anglican Establishment today in our country is inconsistent with the actual state of beliefs in the nation, and a real disadvantage to religion on the whole.'[5] Observe that it was

[1] Cp. Prestige, *Life*, pp. 16f.   [2] *Retrospect*, i. 19.

[3] See *Essays in aid of the Reform of the Church*, ed. by Gore (1898). Cp. p. 142, infra.

[4] *The Basis of Anglican Fellowship*, p. 48.

[5] *The Holy Spirit and the Church*, p. 357.

primarily for the sake of the Church, or in the interests of religion, that Gore wanted Disestablishment. Anyhow he was undoubtedly a Liberal Catholic in the first sense of the term, and we can pass on to the next sense.

It is possible to want liberty *for* the Church without wanting liberty *in* the Church. Indeed, that is now the usual ultramontane position. Gore, on the contrary, was certainly, by profession and intention, a Liberal Catholic in this second sense too, though here there were serious inconsistencies in his position with which we shall have to reckon before we have done.

He stood for various kinds of liberty in the church. He stood for the liberty of each national church to 'develop according to its special temperament a specially characteristic, and therefore an essentially partial, manner of Christian life and manner of holding and teaching Christian truth'.[1] Then, he held that each national church, and especially the Church of England, should 'glory in comprehension'.[2] Given agreement in regard to the fundamental articles of the faith, he said the Church should 'draw lines as seldom as possible'[3] and 'embrace people of very different opinions'.[4] He looked upon the Church of England's emphasis on the authority of scripture as a safeguard of this freedom within the Church. So he spoke of 'a liberal catholicism, a catholicism which limits its properly dogmatic authority carefully and thankfully by the blessed restriction of Scripture'.[5] And again: 'It is [the] appeal to Scripture constantly insisted upon which qualifies the catholicism of the Anglican Church as scriptural or liberal.'[6] Further, in regard to the teaching of the church, Gore protested vigorously against what was, at any rate in his time, the

[1] *Our Place in Christendom*, p. 184.   [2] Ibid.
[3] See Prestige, *Life*, p. 245.   [4] See *Orders and Unity*, p. 150.
[5] Ibid., p. 200.   [6] *The Basis of Anglican Fellowship*, p. 5.

Roman Catholic view that it is the office of the hierarchy to hand out the truth and of the faithful passively to accept it.[1] 'There are not to be two classes in Christianity', he declared, 'one which knows and the other which depends upon them for instruction. All are to know for themselves. . . . All must be trained to exercise their minds. They must not depend on any class of scribes.'[2] He asserted that this liberal or liberating method of teaching was that of our Lord and his apostles. 'I cannot imagine', he said, 'St Paul or St John, or, be it said with reverence, our Lord being jealous of any kind of investigation into the facts of nature or history. . . . The temper encouraged in the New Testament is an eye quite wide-opened to the whole of truth that is really ascertainable and at the same time alive to the limitations of the knowledge of the unseen world which is at present granted to the church.'[3]

You can imagine how appalled Gore would have been by the layman who, after complaining of the prevalence of heresy in modern times, said to the present Bishop of Derby: 'The worst of it is that even in cases in which the clergy believe the right things, you have no guarantee that they are not believing them merely because they happen personally to think them true, instead of accepting them simply and solely upon the authority of Holy Church.'[4] For Gore never tired of claiming for himself as a member of the church the right and the duty to think freely. 'The real Christian', he said, 'will be open to the light whencesoever it comes. In art, in science, in philosophy, in poetry, in all the religions of the world, Christianity will

[1] See, e.g., the words of Pope Pius X quoted in my *Christian Belief and This World*, pp. 76f., and the Pastoral of the English Roman Catholic Bishops, quoted p. 131, *supra*.

[2] *Our Place in Christendom*, pp. 173f.

[3] Ibid., p. 175. Cp. *Catholicism and Roman Catholicism*, p. 30; *The Holy Spirit and the Church*, p. 227.

[4] See A. E. J. Rawlinson, *Catholicism with Freedom* (1922), p. 6.

expect and welcome the light.'[1] In the preface to *Belief in God* he wrote: 'I have, ever since I was an undergraduate, been certain that I must be in the true sense a free thinker, and that either not to think freely about a disturbing subject, or to accept ecclesiastical authority in place of the best judgement of my own reason, would be for me an impossible treason against the light. I must go remorselessly where the argument leads me.'[2]

Moreover, Gore claimed for members of the church freedom not only of thought but of utterance, freedom to speak prophetically. He complained that the tendency of the church had been 'to relegate the prophets to the Old Testament' and observed that established authorities in the church had 'always tended to suspect prophets' but (he said) there is a 'need in every age of prophets, who speak from God simply because they must, to recall men to some forgotten aspect or element of the word of God'.[3] It is the function of the prophet to lead, Gore said. 'The prophet is to lead: the bishop rather to moderate and hold people together, while the prophet agitates them. But he (the bishop) ought to be tolerant of the prophet, and not resent the trouble involved in the stirring of the waters, or be jealous of the superior influence of the unofficial person.'[4]

Gore wrote those words during the period when he was himself a diocesan bishop, and all I have shown so far is that, whatever his own convictions, he professed to be a Liberal Catholic, in that he professed to stand for freedom *within* the church, freedom for prophets and reformers and disturbers of the peace. We now have to ask to what extent he was a Liberal Catholic in the *third* sense of the term. To what extent was he

[1] *The Deity of Christ*, p. 66.

[2] *Belief in God*, p. x. Cp. *The Holy Spirit and the Church*, pp. 188f.; *The Philosophy of the Good Life*, p. 4.

[3] *Orders and Unity*, pp. 157f.   [4] Ibid., p. 159.

a prophet, a reformer or a disturber of the peace himself? In his early days Gore was certainly a reformer and a disturber of the peace in regard to both the doctrine and the order of the Church of England. [I am not attempting to deal here with Gore's teaching and action about social reform and social justice, where his prophetic character was most in evidence; that may indeed be regarded as an aspect of his Liberal Catholicism, but it is so important and distinguishable an aspect that it should be treated as a separate subject.]

Let us begin then with what is at first sight the comparatively simple question of Gore's attitude to the reform of the *order* of the Church of England. He nailed his colours to the mast in 1898 in the volume of *Essays in aid of the Reform of the Church* which he edited and to which he contributed. This volume came out strongly for self-government for the church, as I have already indicated, though not for Disestablishment.[1] But what in retrospect is more striking is the claim that the laity, including women, should be brought to share in the government of the Church as they are said to have done in the first few centuries. Gore himself wrote: 'When a proper ecclesiastical legislature is established with houses of bishops, presbyters, and laity, the laymen should, in the judgement of the present writer, have a veto on any proposed change in the accepted ecclesiastical standards, i.e. on the Book of Common Prayer. No *change* in ecclesiastical formulas or rubrics should be possible against the consent of the laity.'[2] This reform, which has yet to be carried through and which would bring the Church of England into line with other provinces of the Anglican Communion, may very fittingly be described as Liberal Catholic.

But if we turn our attention to other reforms in the ordering

[1] See what H. Scott Holland says in his essay on 'Church and State', op. cit., p. 124.
[2] Op. cit., p. 19.

of the church which Gore persistently urged, we come across what may be a serious flaw or even a basic inconsistency in his Liberal Catholicism. There was in Gore's thought about the church a strain, an essential strain, which moved him to desire much stricter standards of membership and discipline. 'We must', he said, 'prefer reality to numbers', and added: 'I do not doubt that to make church membership real—to insist on a higher standard of church membership—would mean an immense reduction of numbers.'[1] 'It has been our current practice to baptise infants indiscriminately, and, I think, with disastrous results.'[2] These things were said forty years ago. That Gore took this view was doubtless connected with the fact, which Dr Prestige noted, that 'to the end of his life he was insistent on the principle that God works through minorities. To have found himself in a majority might well have caused him both discomfort and misgiving.'[3] If there seems to be an element of perversity in that, it is only fair to add that Gore contended that a church with higher standards of membership, however much smaller in numbers, would 'be much more really useful to the nation as a whole' than the existing church,[4] and also that the kind of freedom which the New Testament reveals is possible only in a church which maintains its standards of membership at a very high level. However true that may be, I think Gore concealed from himself that this strain in his thought really pointed to a sect-type of church or a gathered church which would be inimical to many of the forms of liberty for which as a Liberal Catholic he professed to stand. It may seem paradoxical but I am going to suggest directly that Gore's conception of the church, though High, was not High enough—nor Liberal enough—nor Catholic enough.

But first we must consider whether he was a reformer in

[1] *Our Place in Christendom*, p. 186. [2] Ibid., p. 187.
[3] Prestige, *Life*, p. 20. [4] *Our Place in Christendom*, p. 187.

regard to Christian *doctrine*, for a similar problem arises here too. It was concisely put by Dr S. C. Carpenter when reviewing in *Theology* Prestige's *Life of Gore*. 'Dr Prestige', he said, 'does not reveal—perhaps no one could, because Bishop Gore himself never knew it—how it was that the *Lux Mundi* pioneer became the defender. For defender after 1889, he was.'[1] How was it that Gore, who at the time of *Lux Mundi* did more than anyone to liberalize Catholicism in the Church of England by reforming its attitude to biblical criticism and to the doctrines of Inspiration and Christology—how was it that he became so stabilized in the position he arrived at then that, despite his sincere claim to be constantly rethinking his theology, he did not in fact do anything further than defend with much skill and perseverance a reinterpretation of orthodoxy that seems to have been settled once for all.

A friend who saw much of Gore in his last years made the following comment: 'It was as if the intense conflict of those early days in Oxford had left its mark on a sensitive and highly strung nature so that his mind latterly tended to run into fixed gladiatorial attitudes suitable, let us say, to a battle with a Traditionalist, an encounter with a Darwinian, a deadly grappling with a Papist, and so on. He had been fighting so intensely and on so many different fronts that the alignments almost became established frontiers.'[2] That seems to me a perceptive comment, and it is not incompatible with the suggestion of a 'discerning friend' of Dr Carpenter's that 'Liddon's distress in 1889 was so painful a shock to [Gore] that he developed a sort of Never Again complex, and that his transparently honest answers to his own question "Can we still believe?" were at least partially determined by causes which were unknown to

[1] *Theology*, December 1935, p. 354.

[2] J. Conway Davies, 'Charles Gore: Notes for a Psychological Study 1924-1931' in *Theology*, November 1932, p. 260.

himself'.[1] Dr Albert Mansbridge lent his weighty and sympathetic support to that suggestion.[2]

Anyhow, whatever the explanation be, it is the case that after his early doctrinal reformation, which did so much to liberalize Anglican Catholicism, Gore was never again a reformer in this field. On the contrary, he became the doughtiest opponent of other would-be reformers who, as they thought, wanted to carry further what he had begun. Dr Prestige, in his lectures on Gore as a prophet, said that 'no inconsiderable part of his energies was directed into efforts to persuade the authorities of the Church to set limits to the activities of other prophets, both of the ecclesiastical Right and the ecclesiastical Left, whom he found reason to regard as false prophets'.[3] We must face the incongruous fact that this stalwart professor of a liberal and comprehensive Catholicism wanted a Church that was precisely disciplined, doctrinally and liturgically as well as morally.

We may consider (I do myself) that throughout Gore was *substantially* contending for the fundamentals of the faith, but we must at the same time allow that he did so by methods which were inappropriate in one who professed to be a *Liberal* Catholic, and that some of the arguments he used and some of the outworks he defended could have been abandoned without loss to Christian evidences. Dr Prestige put the case mildly when he said it was doubtful whether Gore 'fully appreciated the force of the objection against re-asserting by mere act of administrative authority what had been questioned by process of intellectual criticism: on his own principles of unfettered enquiry, unsound criticism should be countered and overcome by better criticism'.[4] It is true that as a bishop Gore did not

[1] *Theology*, December 1935, p. 354.
[2] See *E. S. Talbot and C. Gore*, pp. 42, 53.
[3] *The Soul of a Prophet*, p.28.   [4] Ibid., p. 29.

actually prosecute individuals for heresy,[1] but, as Henson pointed out, he applied even more objectionable methods of coercion to incumbents in his diocese whom he deemed to be unsound.[2]

The readiness with which Gore attributed irrational prejudices[3] and indeed insincerity[4] to those with whom he disagreed was often unjust and was certainly illiberal. Many of his admirers felt that, when dealing with critical questions in relation to orthodoxy, he drew distinctions which would not carry the weight he put upon them—distinctions between the authority of Bible and of the creeds, between the authority of one creed and another, between the modes of interpreting different articles in the creeds, and between the mythological elements in the Old and New Testaments.[5]

These incongruities in Gore's position are partly, perhaps principally, to be accounted for by his personal character or temperament and I will say something about that when in a minute or two I ask whether he was a Liberal Catholic in my fourth sense of the term, but I want now to suggest that this High Churchman had in some respects a curiously Low conception of the church. This point was made in effect, though without any overt allusion to Gore, in a sermon by Dr Rawlinson, preached before the University of Cambridge in 1928

[1] See what he says in *The Basis of Anglican Fellowship*, p. 26.

[2] See *Retrospect*, i. 78.

[3] E.g. what he says about the notoriously difficult critical problem of the authorship and historicity of the Fourth Gospel. 'I do myself firmly, and after all examination, believe that it is only at the bottom the refusal of the supernatural which leads to that rejection of St. John's authorship. I think the evidence is fairly overwhelming that the Fourth Gospel was really written by John the Apostle and that you must accept its testimony as John's.' *The Deity of Christ*, pp. 39f. Cp. *Belief in God*, p. 207.

[4] Cp. Henson, *Retrospect*, i. 166.

[5] See, e.g., C. W. Emmet, *Conscience, Creeds and Critics* (1918); cp. J. K. Mozley, *Some Tendencies in British Theology* (1951), pp. 76f.

and subsequently published as a pamphlet. The sermon was a sequel to a speech he had made and published some years previously, in which he had taken the Anglo-Catholics to task for their theological timidity and their nervous fear of liberty in the church. In the university sermon, which was entitled 'Freedom within the church', he said that 'Belief in the principle of liberty does not mean simply belief in the liberty of those with whom one happens to be in personal agreement. It means the refusal to have the church turned into a sect, or administered by methods of discipline analogous to those which obtain in the Church of Rome.'[1]

Dr Rawlinson pointed out that 'the plain man' does commonly think of the church as a sect, as a human organization created for certain legally defined purposes. The plain man argues therefore that, on the analogy of other voluntary societies, the clergy are officials paid to teach certain doctrines and to perform certain rites, and that they have no moral right, so long as they retain their position, either to depart from the doctrines or to introduce innovations in worship. But the plain man is wrong, and Dr Rawlinson opposed to this sectarian and juridical conception of the church the belief that the ultimate church—what, I suppose, you would now call the 'eschatological' church—is the whole redeemed people of God: it is a community *sui generis* which has its *raison d'être* in the saving Acts of God, not in any human contract. The church visible on earth is the temporal manifestation of the ultimate church and the vehicle of its life. 'It is in no sense a society, or group of societies (the preacher said), for which there are analogies of a valid kind in the political sphere. . . . Any and every particular manifestation or expression of the Church . . .—for example, the Church of England—ought . . . to aim at being Catholic, in the sense of being comprehensive

[1] A. E. J. Rawlinson, *Freedom within the Church* (1928), p. 6.

of all that is Christian. It ought to aim at excluding none whom our Lord Jesus Christ would not exclude. It ought to rule out in principle no type of thought or of temperament, and no forms of devotion, which are in any sense genuinely and defensibly Christian.'[1] No doubt there are difficulties in this view of the church also, but it represents a Liberal Catholicism which is free from the incongruities of Gore's position, especially the incongruity of combining the notions of a church and a sect.

I come now to the last sense in which a man may be a Liberal Catholic; that is, is this particular Catholic, whatever his particular opinions, free from fanaticism, generous-minded, and so forth? The answer in Gore's case may already be sufficiently evident. Although he had liberal ideals and was capable of appreciating the liberal virtues, he was not temperamentally or characteristically liberal or liberal-minded.

We are told that when he was Vice-Principal of Cuddesdon he kept a picture of Jowett hanging on his study wall. 'When I feel I am stressing an argument too far', he said, 'I look at Jowett and he pulls me up.'[2] It is significant that he realized he needed such a check. A man of liberal temper is tempted in the opposite direction—namely, to qualify all his arguments over carefully with such expressions as 'possibly', 'perhaps' and 'it may be'. Gore's great strength lay in the fact that he had the dispositions of a confessor and a prophet, and confessors and prophets are very rarely men of a liberal temper. 'Gore's prophetic mission was to stimulate personal decision, both in himself and in his contemporaries.'[3] 'I think', he said, 'that when you get outside the special atmosphere of academic circles, the

[1] *Freedom within the Church*, pp. 6, 10ff.

[2] Prestige, *Life*, pp. 38f. Dr Elliott-Binns (*English Thought 1860-1900*, p. 127) says that Gore *always* kept a portrait of Jowett in his study, but this is to go beyond the only authority that he cites for the statement.

[3] Prestige, *The Soul of a Prophet*, p. 16.

only way in which a Church with a definite message can make itself understood in this world is by enshrining its principles in decisive statements.'[1] He was 'passionately eager to bring others to agree with him';[2] it was not in him to view the issues of belief and unbelief or of right and wrong with a dispassionate liberality. For one thing, he was not endowed with the scepticism which is a condition of this kind of liberality. He did indeed once say that there were men who—for the good of us all—have the vocation to be sceptics,[3] but as regards himself he confessed: 'I have really—to be honest—almost never had difficulties of belief, and it seems to me at this moment difficult to imagine how a good man really doubts our Lord's Godhead—though of course I can understand difficulties as stated piecemeal.'[4] Although Henson said that Gore had a 'subtle' intellect,[5] and Gore himself once quoted with approval Renan's saying that 'la vérité consiste dans les nuances',[6] his strength lay in his impatience with subtlety[7] and in his determination to reach definite conclusions.[8] 'If one thinks a thing is wrong on the whole', he said, 'one must (it seems to me) say it's wrong, and not keep explaining how nearly it approaches to being right.'[9]

We ought to admit that Gore's splendid definiteness and

---

[1] *Crisis in Church and Nation*, p. 22.   [2] Prestige, *Life*, p. 257.

[3] See *Orders and Unity*, p. 230. He was thinking of Henry Sidgwick.

[4] See Prestige, *Life*, p. 126.   [5] *Retrospect*, i. 155.

[6] *Belief in God*, p. 31.

[7] Cp. *The Holy Spirit and the Church*, p. 116: 'I find myself as I read in some modern or hypercritical books murmuring the words of the son of Sirach, "There is an exquisite subtilty, and the same is not just."'

[8] 'He was impatient and suspicious, as of all subjective systems, so of those subtler forms of historical research which seemed to end, and to be satisfied with ending, in unsupported probabilities and indeterminate conjectures. He demanded of history decisions which were definite, even if limited, and rationally supported, even if incomplete.' Prestige, *Life*, p. 129.

[9] See ibid., p. 310.

decisiveness in the proclamation of the gospel and of its moral demands often involved him in simplifications which quite properly offended more liberal and critical minds. There was a streak of fanaticism in his character.[1] What else are we to say of his habit—for it was a habit—of threatening to resign his see when he could not get his way in the councils of the bishops?[2] This was the style of the masterful aristocrat that Gore was, but nothing could be less liberal or more reprehensible, and if he had had to measure himself against a stronger episcopal bench, he would not have got away with it.

It is thus paradoxically the case that the man who did more than anyone else to liberalize the Anglo-Catholic movement, also stimulated in a most illiberal manner what Dr Prestige called the recurring 'touchiness and hypersensitivity'[3] that have marked it ever since Newman's day. The Jerusalem Bishopric, *Essays and Reviews*, the Athanasian Creed, the Deceased Wife's Sister, *Foundations*, the Kikuyu Conference, and even more recent events, have produced conscientious but discreditable manifestations of it. In these so-called crises there have been Anglo-Catholics (and Gore was one of them) who have appeared to suppose that, unless the ark of the covenant was secured by them and in their way, the Lord God would lose control of his church. So, although Gore was entitled to claim that he was a Liberal Catholic in some senses of the term, in this last sense he should not be so described.

That is my concluding point, and it will be clearer if I remind you of Dr Albert Mansbridge's comparison between Gore and E. S. Talbot, in the charming book he wrote about them both. Gore, he says,

[1] Cp. John Gore, *Charles Gore: Father and Son*, p. 74; Henson, *Retrospect*, i. 80, 159.

[2] Henson, op. cit., i. 167, ii. 5.

[3] Prestige, *The Soul of a Prophet*, p. 30.

knew quite well that many of his convictions were held on a balance of evidence, but he held these with as full an assurance as if there were no contrary case to be considered. . . . He had not the temperament of a philosopher. He was not greatly interested in the process of arriving at convictions; it was the convictions themselves that concerned him. . . . Talbot . . . seldom had a well-defined position upon a controversial issue. There might be no doubt on which side of a dividing line his sympathies lay, but he remained vividly aware of the case for other opinions. . . . It was clear to all that at every stage he was thinking through once more the subject under discussion, even welcoming new considerations which called for a complete review of convictions long cherished. He was essentially more liberal-minded than Gore, though less associated in the public mind with opinions of the kind called liberal.[1]

I will end by expressing a settled conviction of my own. It is essential that the church, in particular the Church of England, should hold men of Gore's dogmatic and prophetic disposition, but it would be disastrous if they were ever able to dominate or to dictate to it. When I was a student at Wells Theological College I remember Dr Armitage Robinson saying that he had one axiom about the Church of England which was that it must be kept broad enough to include Dr Rashdall. At the time I was rather shocked, or at least puzzled (it was the time of the Girton Conference controversy), but I am now sure that Armitage Robinson was right and that, in this respect, though I do not say in other respects, he was a better Liberal Catholic—and a better churchman—than Charles Gore.

[1] Mansbridge, E. S. Talbot and C. Gore, p. 88. Cp. ibid., p. 90: 'Gore's mind asked more questions but was restless till they were answered; Talbot rather brooded over the subject and was content that much should be as yet indeterminate.'

VIII

WHAT IS ANGLICANISM?[1]

I

IT is rumoured that some years ago, at an interdenominational conference of theologians held at Bishopthorpe, the Anglican position was best represented by a well-known professor who is a Congregationalist. That report may be apocryphal, but it raises the question: What *is* the Anglican position? My purpose in this essay is—I will not say to supply but—to hint at the true answer to that question. But a good deal of introduction will be necessary in order that we may understand how it comes about that in 1948, about four hundred years after the Reformation, many Anglicans find themselves asking this question without being able to frame the answer clearly, and perhaps with considerable anxiety about what the answer may be, or even whether there is an answer at all.

I ought to say at once that I am going to consider the question in the setting of the Church of England, rather than of the Anglican Communion as a whole. I do this not because I suppose that the Church of England is the purest part, or the most satisfactory specimen, of the Anglican churches, for I hold that in some respects that is far from being the case. I shall speak of the Church of England rather than of the Anglican Communion, because I know the Church of England best, and also because the problem with which I am concerned is a pressing problem here, whatever may be the case elsewhere.

Even those whose knowledge of the Church of England is most remote have some idea that its characteristics are both

[1] Reprinted from *Theology*, June and July, 1948.

peculiar and elusive. He is a bold man who attempts to say precisely what Anglicanism is. And, as a matter of fact, part of what I want to say might be expressed in the assertion that there is no such thing as Anglicanism, though I shall reach a more positive conclusion than that.

There are those who suppose that the peculiar characteristics of the Church of England are the result of the Elizabethan settlement and that their maintenance depends on the continuation of the establishment in England. No doubt it is impossible to explain the character of the Church of England, and also of the Anglican Communion, without reference to the Elizabethan settlement; but the notion that the Anglican character now depends on the English establishment is manifestly absurd, since the establishment subsists in England alone, whereas the Anglican Communion has a more or less similar character in all parts of the world. Nowhere, moreover, has the termination of establishment resulted in a dissolution of the Church into what are alleged to be its constituent and inconsistent parts.

At the same time I want to acknowledge a fact which has not yet received the consideration that it deserves, and sooner or later will require. Post-Reformation Anglican theology developed on the basis of the assumption that the Church of England was a national church—that it was the visible Church of Christ in England. As such it claimed to be a pure and reformed part of the Church Universal. It recognized that there were national churches in other lands, some reformed, some unreformed, but it never supposed that there could be a number of true churches in one land. In England, at all events, those bodies of Christians that were separated from the national church were deemed to be schismatic sects, whether they were Romish or Protestant dissenters. This claim to be the one true church of the nation may still be made with a measure of plausibility in England itself, though it is seldom if ever, now *consistently* made. It was in fact becoming hard to sustain even a hundred years ago.

> A citizen of a large town (wrote James Martineau in 1850) can wander every Sunday into the chapel to hear mass, or into the Friends' meeting-house to keep silence, or into the Wesleyan, or Independent, or Unitarian chapel, to hear in each a different doctrine of nature and of grace, expounded perhaps in a manner quite as edifying as the rector's. How can you persuade that man that Christ has only one church in England?—that the rector is distinguished from all these people, as a divine messenger from a set of impostors?— that he is appointed to open and shut the heavenly kingdom, while they are set for a delusion and a snare?[1]

It was certainly difficult to sustain such a claim then, and it is much more difficult now. And in most of the countries where there are now churches in communion with Canterbury the claim cannot even be made to look plausible. In 1865 Bishop Atkinson of North Carolina spoke of the claim of the Protestant Episcopal Church in the U.S.A. 'to be a pure and vigorous branch of the Church Catholic', adding the hope that it would rise continually 'into wider usefulness and higher influence, until at length it shall become the Church, not merely in the United States, but of the American people'.[2] I suppose no churchman in America who weighed his words, then or now, would venture to say more than that.

It has come about that most Anglicans in England and elsewhere, without realizing what a difference the change makes, now think in terms not of national churches, of which the Church of England is one, but of world denominations, of which the Anglican Communion is one. The change has come about partly as a result of the missionary expansion of the last

---

[1] Martineau, *Miscellanies* (1852), p. 306.

[2] See J. B. Cheshire, *The Church in the Confederate States* (1912), p. 219.

150 years, which has carried the Anglican Communion into countries where a claim to be *the* national church, if it were plainly asserted, would seem preposterous. The long movement towards toleration also led to the gradual replacement of seventeenth-century conceptions of exclusive or inclusive national churches by quite different conceptions of churches as international denominations, and of the Universal Church as a collection of denominations instead of as embodied in national churches. It is obvious that we cannot simply resuscitate seventeenth-century conditions and conceptions. I will only say here that a multiplicity of national churches is much more in accord with the biblical doctrine of the church than a multiplicity of world sects.

The earlier Anglican divines set themselves to show that the Church of England, as it emerged from the upheavals of the Reformation period, was a true church. They had to meet assaults from opposite sides—from Rome and from Geneva, from papists and from puritans. Their method was not to develop a comprehensive system of doctrine, but to defend the comprehensive church order which they had providentially inherited, to defend it on the grounds of its accord with Scripture, primitive antiquity or tradition, and sound reason. The great works of Anglican divinity, such as Hooker's *Ecclesiastical Polity* or Butler's *Analogy*, have been evoked by a contemporary need or challenge, have been written *ad hoc* if not *ad hominem*, and it may be said that to this extent at least the characteristic method of Anglican divinity is biblical. No doubt there have been some Anglican divines who have tried to build theological systems, but they have not been highly esteemed and they are little remembered. Dr Pusey in 1830 wrote to a German correspondent as follows:

You will doubtless have observed that few, if any, of our writings have originated in an abstract love of investigation;

our greatest and some immortal works have arisen in some
exigencies of the times; the writings of Chillingworth,
Hooker, Butler, Bull (and so of the rest) were written not
merely to solve problems of importance in themselves, but
such as the good of the Church in our country at that time
required.[1]

There is no work that has played a part in Anglican divinity
corresponding to the parts played elsewhere by Calvin's
Institutes or the *Summa* of St Thomas.

Nor have Anglicans regarded this fact as a deficiency or as a
matter for apology (unless it be in quite recent times). We
found that we had all that was needed for the practical purposes of a living church in the Bible, the Creeds and the Book
of Common Prayer. And until the nineteenth century we had
as well a traditional body of divinity which was generally read
and studied. I do not wish to suggest that the averge parson in
in the eighteenth century spent two or three hours a day in
reading our standard divines. I suspect that there was much
truth then, as there is now, in an observation which Hugh
James Rose made to Newman in 1836: 'I consider the English
as an eminently anti-reading nation, and . . . of course the
Clergy partake of this character.'[2] Still, it is true that until the
nineteenth century Anglicans had common ground, since in
so far as they read at all they read the same authors, although
they treated no single author as authoritative in the way that
Lutherans treat Luther. It did not occur to anyone to formu-
late, let alone to answer, the question: What is Anglicanism?
Anglicans knew well enough their tradition and their direction,
and felt no need to encase their faith or their church in an
elaborate system of doctrine. According to the *Oxford English
Dictionary* the earliest use of the word 'Anglicanism' is in

[1] See Liddon's *Life of Pusey*, i. 238.
[2] See Burgon's *Lives of Twelve Good Men* (1888), i. 209.

1846,[1] whereas the word 'Presbyterianism' dates from the seventeenth century, and that is significant.

Various circumstances within and without the Church of England, which I will specify, have, however, made the question, 'What is Anglicanism?' almost a burning one in some circles today.[2] First, the development in the Church of England of at least three organized parties, each of which has seemed to stand for a different system of doctrine. It is true that previously there were different schools of thought in the Church, as indeed there always will be in any Christian body that is more than a sect. But up till the nineteenth century High Churchmen, Latitudinarians, etc., all regarded their primary allegiance as being due to the Church of England itself, and not to a party. What distinguished them was a particular emphasis in their interpretation of the teaching of the church, divergent pastoral methods, or a particular political affiliation. In any case, there was no question of the elaborate party *organizations* which have since become familiar. By the end of the nineteenth century, however, it came about that there were many loud-voiced members of the church who regarded themselves primarily as adherents of Evangelicalism or Anglo-Catholicism or Broad Churchmanship, who were almost accidentally, or at least secondarily, members of the Church of England. It became apparent that the parties stood for different systems and incompatible systems, and therefore the question arose: What does the Church of England stand for? Is it anything more than a device for keeping in uneasy juxtaposition a number of sects, parties or systems that do not really belong

[1] The word *anglicanisme* occurs in Lamennais' *Essai sur l'indifférence* (1817), i. 158. 'Anglicanism' was spoken of by Newman in 1841, see his *Essays and Sketches*, ed. by C. F. Harrold (1948), ii. 160.

[2] Some of the points in the following paragraphs I have already made in an abbreviated form in my Hale Lectures. See *The Theology of F. D. Maurice* (1948), Chapter viii.

together? At a time when party hostility in the church was at its height, James Martineau put the case in these vigorous terms:

> The Act of Uniformity (which, of course, includes the Prayer Book), it is now confessed, enforces a heterogeneous congeries of theological propositions with no organic unity, held together by no higher bond than the printer's frame of types, and incapable of coexisting in any mind of logical grasp and moral earnestness to use it; and the only uniformity which it secures among the clergy, beyond the weekly monotony upon the ear, is that of invariable self-contradiction, of partial unveracity, and bitter mutual aversions.[1]

This, then, is one circumstance that has led members of the Church of England to ask with considerable anxiety: What is Anglicanism?

(Before I continue I would remark that the picture of the . Church of England as a congeries of warring sects has in point of fact always been misleading. While the church as a whole has not been unaffected or uninfluenced by the various parties that have been formed within it, there has been a solid and central mass of Anglicans who have never been in any of the parties, but who have maintained the unhyphenated allegiance to the Church of England itself which was traditional with their forefathers. This is probably true of a large majority of the clergy, and certainly of the bulk of the laity. I do not know that these are much worried today by the question: What is Anglicanism? It is rather the unsettled remainders of the parties that are now in their decadence who are agitated by this question.)

A second general circumstance that has prompted the question is a result of the disintegrating effects of what is called modern thought upon all traditional theology. As I have said,

[1] *Miscellanies*, p. 414.

until the last century Anglicans were accustomed to read the works of their standard divines in so far as they were accustomed to read any divinity at all, and this gave them a common universe of discourse and theological perspective.[1] This was true of the educated laity as well as of the clergy. I possess an abridgment of Hooker's *Ecclesiastical Polity*, published in 1773, *adapted to the use of families*, as the title-page says. But during the Liberal period it came to be supposed that seventeenth- and eighteenth-century divinity, and indeed any divinity more than a generation old, must be obsolete. Gradually the custom of reading our standard divines died out. I believe that in most English dioceses (I know of only one exception) Hooker disappeared from the syllabus of reading required from candidates for ordination about twenty years ago; some years before, Paley had been at last retired from little-go at Cambridge.

I fear it may now be the case that only a small proportion of the clergy has read any divinity to speak of that was published before the beginning of this century. And twentieth-century Anglican divines have themselves been for the most part individual essayists rather than reinterpreters of a theological tradition in which they had deep roots. It may appear that Oxford philosophical idealism or historical positivism rather than the Bible and the Prayer Book has provided the ground and determined the method of their teaching, though the fact that they were still tied to the use of the Bible and the Prayer Book prevented their departure from Scripture and tradition from being as manifest, or indeed as real, as otherwise would have been the case. Too many present-day Anglicans might be described by some words which I came across in the Journals of Caroline Fox. Caroline mentions a visit which she

[1] For a remarkable example of a course of reading undertaken by a young clergyman early in the nineteenth century, see W. R. W. Stephens' *Life and Letters of Dean Hook* (1878), pp. 64f.

paid to a Moravian lady named Schimmelpenninck, whom she thus describes: 'She is a very genial person, so alive to the beauty of all Religious Faith, however widely diverse. She spoke of having suffered from an indiscriminate theological education.' Anyhow, this severence from traditional moorings, in a period of inevitable intellectual upheaval, is a second circumstance which has led theological students to ask with particular, and sometimes poignant, anxiety: What is Anglicanism?

But even if this inquiry had not been pressed upon them by the internal condition of Anglican theology it would have been pressed upon them by the general theological environment of the present time, and this constitutes a third circumstance. The easy-going confidence which most of us had in a more or less liberal and eclectic theology was first surprised and then shaken when we learned that in Germany, which used to be the spearhead of Liberalism, and elsewhere on the Continent a violent reaction had occurred. A little later we learned that the churches on the Continent were being driven to make a confessional stand and that they were again taking very seriously their traditional standards. It appeared that the Lutherans and Calvinists, about whom we knew very little, as well as the Romanists, about whom we knew a good deal, were discovering in their respective traditions theological resources which enabled them to make declarations of principle on the basis of which their resistance to totalitarianism and other forms of modern infidelity rested. Anglicans have been beginning to wonder whether they have any corresponding traditional resources upon which they will be able to call in the struggle that may be impending for them too, and upon which they ought perhaps to be calling already. You can see that this gives further point to the question: What is Anglicanism?

Another circumstance, connected with but distinct from that

which I have just mentioned, arises from the intellectual confusion, not to say chaos, of the age, which causes those who
become aware of it and anxious to get out of it or over it, to
look for some definite, dogmatic and forthright faith, for
some systematic framework for thought and action from
within which they can at any rate achieve a consistent criticism
of other people, even if they cannot construct much themselves. Here we have to admit that the Romanists in the
Thomist or neo-Thomist system and the neo-orthodox Protestants in what is roughly called Barthianism seem at first to
have an advantage. Anglicans have nothing to offer so massive,
so compact or so definite. It is therefore not surprising that
some of our brightest and perhaps best young divines have
been resorting to one or other, and occasionally both, of those
schools and attempting to develop an Anglican version of
neo-Thomism or of neo-Calvinism. Both projects can be
represented as a resumption of the right and original course of
Anglican divinity, since divines like Hooker were greatly
indebted to and influenced by both St Thomas and Calvin. A
partisan theologian with some skill and little scrupulousness
can so emphasize and isolate the Catholic or Protestant strain
in Anglican divinity, and ignore what is inconvenient for his
thesis, as to make its characteristic tradition appear to be either
purely Catholic or purely Protestant. Few of us now, as I have
indicated, are sufficiently acquainted with the whole corpus of
our traditional divinity readily to check these brave and
ingenious essays; and the truth is further obscured by the way
in which our formularies have been industriously glossed by
one school and another. But we may have a shrewd suspicion
that these essays are *tours de force*, and that the gist of the matter
is being left out. They are really marginal manœuvres which
may serve to direct attention to, as well as to divert attention
from, the main battle front: by which I mean the real question

which the existence of the Church of England imposes on its own members and brings before Christendom in a tangible and practical, not merely a theoretical, form.

II

The question is whether a church, I should say the church, can be, and if so ought to be, both Catholic and Protestant. In the remainder of this essay I want to go some way towards showing what this question means. For obviously, thus stated, it begs many questions. Not least: What is meant by the words 'Catholic' and 'Protestant' in this context? The word 'Catholic' is not used here in its primary and fundamental sense, which is that of the creed, but as pointing to one of two recognizably different types of Christian tradition and institution which have been familiar in the West since the Reformation. An ecclesiastically unsophisticated visitor from the European Continent, upon making his first acquaintance with the Church of England, will be puzzled to know to which type it belongs, and as his acquaintance becomes closer and deeper his perplexity may increase.

For, on the one hand, he will discover that the present-day Church of England not only claims, but displays many ostensible signs to support its claim, to be continuous with the pre-Reformation *Ecclesia Anglicana*, and in fact to be the same *Ecclesia Anglicana*, purged of medieval corruptions, and brought into line with scriptural and primitive standards. The least significant of these signs is the church's tenure of the ancient cathedrals and parish churches. It is more significant that the cathedrals and parish churches are used for the same purposes as they ever were. Bishops are still enthroned in the cathedrals, and parish ministers are called priests and exercise priestly functions. As regards that, let me cite once more the disinterested witness of James Martineau:

The sacerdotalism of the English Church (he said) is as absolute as that of the Roman. It matters little whether the sacraments be more or fewer; whether their *modus operandi* be a little more subjective or a little more objective; whether the right to absolve be used with the healthy or only with the sick, so long as a ritual purification of human nature is pronounced indispensable, and the patent-right to effect it is conceded by a *jus divinum* to a certain body of men, the whole mischief of the Papal scheme remains.[1]

It is true that the cathedrals and parish churches are commonly furnished in a less ornate and colourful manner than they were in the Middle Ages or are on the European Continent today, though they are kept in a much tidier and cleaner condition. Anyhow, the point is that from the baptism of infants to the obsequies of the departed they are used for the purposes for which they were built.

The Church of England has a liturgy, a 'Book of Common Prayer'. Its liturgy is a simplified and amended form of what was traditional in Western Christendom, the amendments having been designed to bring it into accord with the canons of the ancient fathers. Again, the traditional Christian year— the calendar of feasts and fasts, of saints' days and holy days— continues to be observed, though also in a simplified form. The same creeds are recited, the same sacraments are administered, the same orders of the ministry are perpetuated, and great importance seems to be attached both in the church's ordinal and in its practice to the maintenance of episcopal ordination, although the church's divines hold various opinions about why this should be so. The hierarchical and synodical structure of the church is in principle the same as it ever was (still all too feudal, some would say), though it has been expanded and reshaped to meet new needs. From these and other appearances

[1] *Miscellanies*, p. 408.

our continental visitor would infer that the Church of England is 'Catholic'.

On the other hand, he would find also plenty of no less unmistakable signs that it is 'Protestant'. Whatever a section of its members may have said during the last hundred years, the Church of England implicitly glories in the Reformation. Like other reformed churches, it rejects unequivocally the papal claims as they were asserted at the time of the Reformation, and still more as they have been developed since. It does not claim infallibility. ('Two things', said Hooker, 'there are which greatly trouble these later times: one that the Church of Rome cannot, another that Geneva will not, err.') The Church of England's formularies and traditional divinity bear unambiguous testimony to the cardinal Reformation principle of justification by faith. Though it values tradition more than other reformed churches and explicitly appeals to the authority of 'the catholic fathers and ancient bishops', it has ever stood for the open Bible, for 'the sufficiency of the holy Scriptures for salvation', and in its public worship, while it provides for more preaching than any other 'Catholic' church, it reads more of the Bible each year than any other 'Protestant' church. 'We use the Bible itself more frequently in our service than all the Protestant sects and all the Reformed churches together,' said F. D. Maurice.[1]

That will suffice to indicate the Catholic and Protestant signs that the Church of England bears upon its face. And the question is: Are these the signs of a true church, or the results of an indefensible compromise? The question is whether a true church ought to bear witness in its doctrine, its ordinances, its structure and its discipline, to both Catholic and Protestant principles—whether at the time of the Reformation the truth lay neither with Rome nor with Geneva, but somewhere

[1] *The Kingdom of Christ* (1838), ii. 239.

between or apart from them, and *mutatis mutandis* does so still? Or would an honest and intelligent Anglican perceive that he was faced by the predicament which was thus described by James Bryce in a letter that he wrote to a friend in 1864:

> No man can logically be an Anglican at all, but must either trust himself far more boldly to the conclusions of human reason, as Protestantism in its genuine forms does, or else fling himself with eyes tight shut into the bosom of an infallible church.[1]

Is that the ineluctable dilemma which the Church of England is trying to evade?

Observe that the question is not whether a true church can or may contain some members who are or profess to be 'Catholics' and others who are or profess to be 'Protestants', and who for some reason or other agree to live in the same house without really cohabiting. That would be only a parody of a church. In these latter days the conception of Anglican comprehensiveness has been taken to mean that it is the glory of the Church of England to hold together in juxtaposition as many varieties of Christian faith and practice as are willing to agree to differ, so that the church is regarded as a sort of league of religions. I have nothing to say for such an unprincipled syncretism. This debased conception of comprehensiveness has no sanction in our traditional standards, in our classical divines, or in the official witness of the church today.

Samuel Wilberforce was on the Anglican spot when he asked himself in 1838: '*Quaere*, have I hardness enough not to be ground to powder between the Evangelical and Newman mills?'[2] The principle of comprehension is that a church ought to hold the fundamentals of the Faith and at the same time allow for differences of opinion and of interpretation in

[1] See H. A. L. Fisher, *James Bryce* (1927), i. 76.
[2] See A. R. Ashwell, *Life of Samuel Wilberforce* (1880), i. 136.

secondary matters, especially rites and ceremonies. It is this principle that excluded, if I may put it so, those who believed too little, for instance any who did not accept the creeds, as well as those who believed too much, for instance those who held that submission to the Bishop of Rome is necessary to salvation, or that Holy Scripture requires the presbyterian form of church government and permits no other. Within those limits, which were secured by a uniform liturgy and by Articles of Religion which purported to be positive where Scripture was positive and reticent where it was not, it allowed for the maximum of flexibility and variety.

It would seem, then, that the proper and distinctive task of Anglican theologians is to show, if it can be shown, that this principle is of permanent validity, though of changing application, and that it is upon this principle that the whole church ought again to be brought into visible unity. But it is a task from which modern Anglican divines have let themselves be a good deal distracted—excusably so, perhaps, in view of the number of fronts on which a modern divine is expected to fight, or at least to dawdle. What is distinctive of the Church of England is not a theological system, not an 'ism nor a collection of 'isms, but a theological method or direction. We ought not to try to reproduce or treat as permanently binding the teaching of our sixteenth- or seventeenth-century divines, but to study the method—their appeal to and use of Scripture, tradition and reason—by which they rejected Tridentine Catholicism and pure Calvinism, and to use that method today in examining and assessing Ultramontanism, neo-Calvinism and other contemporary systems. Anglican theology is true to its genius when it is seeking to reconcile opposed systems, rejecting them as exclusive systems, but showing that the principle for which each stands has its place within the total orbit of Christian truth, and in the long run is secure only within that orbit or (in the idiom of today) when it is held in tension with other apparently opposed, but really complementary, principles.

For example, the principle of justification by faith is fundamental, and we find it acknowledged by St Thomas Aquinas as well as by all the Reformers. But when, as in Lutheranism, it is made the basis of an exclusive system and everything seems to be built upon it alone, and the salvation promised to men here and now is apparently made to consist solely in the forgiveness of sin, then we must insist that sanctification is also a fundamental principle equally rooted in the biblical testimony, and that salvation means present incorporation into the mystical body of Christ and growth in holiness. Post-Tridentine Catholicism, while it has affirmed this latter principle, as Lutheranism has not, and has much to teach us about it, yet has also greatly erred by turning it into an elaborate system in which justification by faith is soft-pedalled and in effect denied by legalizing the Christian life and by separating moral from ascetic theology. We must, of course, admit that the Church of England has failed to bear adequate witness in practice to both the principles which it professes and to the reconciliation of which it is committed. Nevertheless, we shall not redress our failure by embracing either the Lutheran or the Ultramontane system, but by holding together the principles for which in this connexion each stands, and which, as developed into separate systems, distort the balance of the Faith.

This was the method both of our Thirty-nine Articles and of our standard divines, pursued in relation to the controversies of the period, and it is not difficult to see that the same method has been, and may again be, fruitfully applied to other perennial antitheses—for instance, those between creation and redemption, between revelation and reason, between the Bible and the Church, between the ministry of the word and of the sacraments, between world-affirmation and world-denial, between authority and freedom, and so forth. I am very far from saying that the method of reconciling apparent opposites can be or has been followed only by Anglican divines. Quite the contrary: it is a method that can be followed by divines anywhere in the universal church, and in every church there have been divines who have followed it. Thus it is quite possible that a non-Anglican divine did represent the Anglican position at Bishopthorpe better than any of the Anglicans who were present. Perhaps the greatest theologians have all aimed at the reconciliation of contraries, and it is the camp followers who turn a many-sided into a one-sided divinity. As John Stuart Mill said, 'In the human mind, one-sidedness has always been the rule, and many-sidedness the exception.'[1]

If this be so, the most hopeful feature of the present theological landscape is the coming together of theologians who have been nurtured in different traditions and in different systems, and their edifying preference for listening to and learning from one another to refuting one another. It would be ridiculous for Anglicans to claim any monopoly of this admirable disposition. Rather, they should be thankful that, while they have nothing so impressive to point to as the great systems in which other traditions have originated or culminated, providence has assigned to them the modest role through these last centuries of witnessing, often no more than mutely, that the proponents of these systems are brethren in Christ, and that their principles, despite their rival systems, are reconciled in what F. D. Maurice called the constitution of the kingdom of Christ.

It is necessary to add that a theology of reconciliation or of comprehension does not mean a theology of moderation, of the *juste milieu*, of sitting on the fence, of nerveless indecision.

[1] *On Liberty*[3] (1864), p. 83.

168

That is what it may rot away into. But, rightly understood and in its genuine representatives, it is a theology not of fog or haze, but of thunder and lightning; a theology which comes down off the fence, but not always on the same side, and which certainly does not fall into a copy-book place on a party line. It is a theology, of which you can never feel that you know just what it is going to do or say next—which is what I always do feel both about the theologies of a party and about the theology of moderation.

If it be granted, then, that we ought to pursue a theology of reconciliation, we shall need always to be on our guard against its characteristic corruptions. A theology of reconciliation is very easily degraded. It lends itself to the natural ambitions of a vicar of Bray and is liable to be exploited by more august time-servers. Sentimentalists and opportunists can use its language. A saying like 'life is greater than logic' can be used as a pretext for shoddy thinking, the evasion of difficulties, and all kinds of superficiality. Even its best and sincerest adherents may acquire demoralizing habits and pursue unprincipled tactics, preferring peace before truth and putting safety first. Bishop Hensley Henson wrote of Archbishop Randall Davidson: 'The life-long habit of "getting round" difficulties, instead of facing them, hardly prepares a man for the handling of a crisis.'[1] And again: 'Unfortunately, his Grace has an inveterate habit of adding qualifications to every apparently clear declaration, until the final impression left is entirely different from that originally made.'[2] In short, ecclesiastical statesmen, whose aim is to maintain an equilibrium, are inclined to cloak their designs in a theology of reconciliation, and so to discredit it.

The leaders of the Church of England are probably not as much aware as they need to be of this their peculiar peril. Still,

[1] Henson, *Retrospect of an Unimportant Life* (1943), ii. 183.
[2] Ibid., ii. 203.

it looks now as though crises of one kind or another—and the presence in our church of theological fanatics of one kind or another—will put a stop to the most ingeniously contrived and persistently maintained equilibrium. It looks as though we are coming to a point where we must either reconcile or perish, and where we must either show that the principle of comprehension is true and not merely Anglo-Saxon, or be driven from it.

Bishop Whipple of Minnesota, preaching before the Lambeth Conference of 1888,[1] coined the phrase 'the Church of the Reconciliation' to describe the united church to which he looked forward. Perhaps it is a title that indicates better than any other what is the Anglican position, and I would add that we should feel committed not only to the reconciliation of the Catholic and Protestant traditions in the West, but also of the Eastern and Western traditions and to the reconciliation of the age-long faith with new discoveries and modes of thought. But only if we are continually being reconciled among ourselves can we hope to perform what seems to be the distinctive mission of the Anglican Communion, namely to call all Christians into unity upon the principle of comprehension.

[1] See R. T. Davidson, *The Lambeth Conferences of 1867, 1878 and 1888* (1889), p. 246.

IX

THE APPALLING
RELIGIOUSNESS OF AMERICA

Note. At the end of a three-months' visit to the U.S.A. in 1947, I was asked
by Dr Reinhold Niebuhr, the Editor of *Christianity and Crisis*, to contribute
to that journal an account of some of my impressions. I was rash enough
to do so, and on my return to England published the article in *Theology* as
well. I still think that the points I made in this piece of journalism were
of more than local or ephemeral interest.

An invitation to one who is visiting the United States
for the first time, and who has been here for less
than three months, to give his impressions of religion in America is an invitation to him to make a
fool of himself, though I acquit the editor of having that
design upon me. I have been no farther West than Chicago,
and no farther South than Washington, D.C. I know that there
are vast areas not only of American territory but of American
life and religion of which I have seen nothing, though I have
been told much about them, enough to warn me that any
generalization about this variegated and complex scene must
be risky. Moreover, although as I have travelled about I
seem to have seen an immense amount in a short time, yet I
have been located chiefly in colleges and seminaries and in
church circles. It is true that I have learned a considerable
amount about other aspects of American life, and have been
present both at the World Series[1] and at a banquet of indus-
trialists! Still, my impressions are bound to be partial and
superficial; I have myself come across many exceptions to
what I am going to say, and I can myself think of many ways

[1] The World Series is the culmination of the baseball season, and means
much more to the U.S.A. than the Cup Final and the Boat Race combined
mean to England.

in which my observations might be qualified. But while I am making a fool of myself, I may as well do so boldly. Nor will I occupy space in saying how uniformly charming and hospitable I have found Americans to be. Not the least engaging of your characteristics is your eagerness to hear yourselves candidly criticized.

Religion versus God.—The first thing that has struck me is that America is now much more religious than Britain. People here go to church much more, and I am told that church attendance has tended to increase since the end of the war. Your churches appear to be flourishing institutions, and they strike me, even if they do not strike you, as fabulously opulent. Our churches in Britain, on the other hand, are all more or less impoverished and tottering, and are on the verge of economic bankruptcy. At first sight the comparative prosperity of religion in America is calculated to hearten and gratify a visiting clergyman or to make him envious. But on second thoughts I find it curiously depressing.

It reminds me of the prodigious religiousness of Britain in the nineteenth century, the aftermath of which I can myself remember in the days of my childhood before 1914. That religiousness, all that business and efficiency in organizing religious services and activities, served, I am sure, as a cushion against the hard impact of the living God. Our churches were like comfortable and well-managed religious clubs, in which we felt nicely at home, in which we felt good, in which we even wanted to be better, at least on Sunday evenings when singing particularly lush hymns. Although you do not go to church on Sunday evenings, your churches remind me of all that.

In Britain this religious efficiency and prosperity is being dissolved, where it has not already been dissolved, but out of the dissolution or in the midst of it the voice of the living God is beginning to be heard again, scaring and confounding us and making us feel most uncomfortable. As the cushion of religion, with which we were able to keep God at a respectable distance, collapses, we are beginning to turn to our Bibles in quite a fresh frame of mind, and its mighty words about the majesty and the wrath and the mercy of God, which in the old days of security we had got pleasantly muffled, are piercing us with their terror and their glory. Thus in Britain, while our churches are metaphorically if not literally falling into ruin, the disturbing and restoring presence of the living God is becoming an experienced reality amid the ruins. Here in the U.S.A., it seems to me, the cushion of religious efficiency and prosperity is still doing its comfortable, but fatal, work. I can only record this impression. It is not for me to say what those of you who are aware of this condition, as I know some of you are, can do about it. In the end, this is a matter wherein we have in agony to beseech God to show us what *he* is going to do about it.

Sect versus Church.—The second thing that has struck me is your sectarianism. Observe that I say your sectarianism, not your sects, about which I knew plenty before I came here, more than I have been able to see since I came. Moreover, the old distinction between a church and a sect is now much confused everywhere. There are great churches which are riddled with sectarianism, and there are little sects which have the outlook and the accent of a great church. Nor do I wish to suggest that we are free from sectarianism in Britain. Far from it. But here it seems to be carried to its logical limit and to become fully explicit. And I will confess that it strikes me as a very horrid thing. The fact that you have so many churches and sects is, I realize, due in the first instance to the variety in the forms of Christianity which emigrants from Europe brought with them. I am not saying that Americans are to be blamed either for this original circumstance or for its present-day consequences.

What surprises and shocks me is your apparent blindness to the flat contradiction between a collection or even a federation of sects and the fundamental idea of Christ's Church. I attribute this blindness to your familiarity with, and necessary acquiescence in, this babel of church sects. Your churches, despite the splendid and universal professions which they may enshrine in their creeds or formularies, seem complacently to regard it as their task to cater for the religious needs of such individuals or such sections of the population as will patronize them. I see no body (certainly not the large but Rome-dominated and exclusive popish sect) standing forth and bearing witness that the work of Christ in every land is to bind men together in one universal family or kingdom without regard to their different racial origins, trades and professions, income brackets, class interests, political parties, etc.

I find that the word 'parish' is used here to denote, not a territorial area and all the people in it, but a gathered congregation; and this is significant. The true idea of a parish church is that it claims all the people dwelling in a particular urban or rural area as citizens of the kingdom of Christ, just as a National Church[1] makes the same claim upon all the members of a nation, whether or not they themselves confess Christ as their King.

In England and Scotland we still have parishes and National Churches in this sense, although the Church of England and the Church of Scotland differ in their forms of government

[1] By a National Church I do not mean a State Church or an Established Church. I do not mean the old pre-toleration type of National Church which was involved in the attempts of civil governments to enforce religious uniformity upon their subjects. I mean a church which realizes its responsibility to God for the whole people in which it is set, in particular its responsibility for binding them into unity on the ground of their membership in Christ's universal body.

and in their relation to the State, although neither has the active allegiance of more than a minority of the population, and although both are accompanied by dissenting sects which they rightly acknowledge to be churches as well as sects. Dreadfully as our Christian and ecclesiastical condition has deteriorated, witness is still borne in our land to the great idea of an inclusive National Church, and the day is perhaps much nearer than any of us realize when the sectarianism which has infected our churches as well as our sects will be transcended in a united Church which will be able to embrace within one body all confessing Christians.

What surprises and shocks me here is not that the U.S.A. recognizes no National Church—for I can perfectly well see that this is not a present possibility—but that the principle of a National Church in all its bearings seems never to have occurred to American Christians as a fundamental criterion which explains your ecclesiastical diseases. You seem to have no higher notion of church union than a federation of sects. I shall be happy to learn that I am mistaken about this.

Law versus Gospel.—But what shocks me most of all is the character of the preaching that seems to prevail in your churches, though here at least I know that there are notable exceptions. So far as I can ascertain, the paradigm of American preaching is: 'Let me suggest that you try to be good.' Moralistic homilies are still the order of the day. They are delivered, no doubt, with various degrees of eloquence, and they may recommend various degrees and forms of virtue or of piety. There may even be such preachers with fire in their bellies, though I have not come across them.

Preachers take texts from Scripture (though they do not always do that much), and treat them as mottoes or captions under which they excogitate some religious or moral lessons that have little, if any, direct relation to the Scripture they

have quoted. Who preaches sermons that are genuine exposi-
tions of the text and sense of Scripture, bringing to bear the
great biblical themes of God's judgment and mercy upon men
who are dead in their complacency, self-confidence, or pride?
Your preachers, it seems to me, are still advocating justification
by good works of one kind or another (they may be very
orthodox or very Catholic good works); they are not proclaiming the gospel of salvation by faith in Jesus Christ. They
are not exposing the basic human predicament—namely, that
the attempt to justify ourselves by good works inflates our pride
so that our progress in health turns into a worse disease. This
predicament being unrealized, there is blindness to the starting-
point of the gospel of the New Covenant. You are still preaching the law, and a pretty easygoing or romantic law at that.

These are, I hope you will believe, the faithful wounds of a
friend, who speaks not out of strength but out of weakness,
and who also has Pelagianism in his blood, but who by the
mercy of God has been brought to see it for what it is.

X

THE OBEDIENCE OF A
CHRISTIAN INTELLECTUAL[1]

THE Oxford English Dictionary defines 'an intellectual' as a person possessing, or supposed to possess, superior powers of intellect. Those of whom St Paul speaks in I Cor. 12.8 were intellectuals: 'To one is given through the Spirit the word of knowledge.' In our society the class of intellectuals includes men and women who teach in universities and schools, authors and journalists, poets and artists, the members of the professions described as learned, and others in all walks of life not easily specified who live by the possession of knowledge.

We are to consider what particular things can be said about the way in which intellectuals ought to obey God and consecrate their gifts to his service, having in mind the peculiar talents which they possess and the special temptations to which they are exposed. We shall not attempt to distinguish between the different occupations in which intellectuals are engaged. The suggestions that will be made here concern the obligations and temptations which belong to intellectuals as a class. We can set them out in a series of statements about 'the good Christian intellectual' accompanied by a commentary.

THE GOOD CHRISTIAN INTELLECTUAL IS A MEMBER OF A LOCAL CHURCH

A local church means a worshipping community which draws its members from a locality, e.g. a parish, and is therefore as mixed in its membership as the inhabitants of the

[1] Reprinted from The Christian News-Letter, 30 October 1946.

locality—and not from an institution, e.g. a school, to which
in the nature of the case only a section of society can belong.
The idea of a local church (how far it is realized at present is
another question) is that of a body of all sorts of men, women
and children who happen to live in one place. The bond that
unites them is their humanity, and not the fact that they do the
same work, or enjoy the same recreations, or hold the same
political or religious opinions, or share the same tastes. Those
things split people up into sections according to their peculiari-
ties; the local church binds them all together on the ground
of what they have in common, namely their humanity,
of which Christ is the universal Head. The local church is
indeed the Body of Christ in miniature, or it is (as according
to one interpretation St Paul says in I Cor. 12.27) *a* Body of
Christ.

For this reason all good Christians recognize that it is both
their obligation and their privilege to belong to a local church.
But the obligation has to be particularly pressed upon the
Christian intellectual because he may be tempted either by his
circumstances or by his tastes to disregard it. Thus, if he is a
teacher in a school or college, which has a chapel of its own,
he is inclined to regard that as the centre or focus of his membership in the Church, and within limits it is right that he
should do so. But it is a limited and sectional kind of church
membership. He ought to attach at least equal importance to
the local church in whose life he can actively participate only
in the holidays or during vacations, for that will bring home
to him the fact that to be a Christian is to belong not to a society
of scholars, but to a body of human beings. Or again, if our
intellectual is an independent man of letters, he will be tempted,
instead of participating in the life of the local church round the
corner, to go further afield in search of a church or chapel
which specially caters for him and the likes of him, and where

the services and the preaching may be more agreeable or at least less offensive to his aesthetic sensibilities. If so, he will in effect be looking for a church which is a company of intellectuals, and not (what a church should be) a home for human beings.

Membership in a local church is not only of obligation for intellectuals as for other Christians, but it is calculated to do intellectuals a special kind of good. Their besetting temptation is pride; it is their office to be critical and fastidious. They are almost bound to fancy that they are superior to the rest of mankind, a class apart or above, even though the vulgar crowd is too dull to see it. Active membership in a local church is a continual corrective of this silly, but subtle, arrogance. There the intellectual is made to realize that he is, like the factory-worker or the farm-labourer, simply a member of the Body of Christ. Moreover, having to rub up against ordinary, non-intellectual human beings in the local church and its social life will have a wholesome and humanizing effect on the intellectual, will draw him out of refined cliques, and require him to take part in the elemental human joys and in the elemental human rows! And again and again he will be kept humble as he realizes that very simple people often possess an intuitive wisdom which he with all his pretensions cannot compass, and a generosity towards one another which shames his meanness towards his intellectual colleagues or competitors.

THE GOOD CHRISTIAN INTELLECTUAL PRAYS

Like all other men he is made for eternal life. 'And this is eternal life, that they know thee the only true God, and Jesus Christ whom thou hast sent.' The knowledge of God, which by his mercy is a present possibility and a present fact, binds men together; it is open to all; it is intended for all. Like membership in the local church it brings men into unity, whereas the specialized knowledge of intellectuals, whether it be of mathematics or metallurgy or jurisprudence, separates them from their fellows, even from their fellow intellectuals. The knowledge of God, which unites men, is not allegiance to a theistic philosophy nor even comprehension of Christian doctrine (in these matters men must differ indefinitely), but it is the knowledge of *God*; it is knowing the living God and the living Christ who is the mediator between God and man.

This personal or direct knowledge of God is given to men in all sorts of ways, and to some men who seldom if ever formally pray it may be given quite intimately. Nevertheless, it is normally through praying that the knowledge of God, which is eternal life, becomes articulate, conscious, definite. In the activity of prayer it grows and is enriched. The intellectual needs to pray as much as anyone else, and probably more, because his preoccupation with arguments and systems of thought, and his over-exercise of his creative or critical faculties, incline him to substitute dead or abstract idols of the intellect for personal communion with the living God. Unless he prays regularly, he may find that he knows a great deal about the arguments for the existence of God without knowing God at all, or a great deal about the literary criticism of the Gospels without knowing Jesus Christ as the daily bearer of good news to himself.

But under modern conditions it is no easier for the average intellectual than for anyone else to find time for prayer. Intellectuals are caught up in the general busy-ness of modern society. Official duties absorb their energies; they hurry from one engagement to another; and when they are at home many of them have to spend a lot of time over domestic chores, which until a generation ago servants did for them.

These facts must be faced. They are not faced in the classical literature about prayer and the spiritual life, for the perfectly good reason that they did not then exist. It must be added that they do not seem always to be faced by contemporary preachers and writers who in their instructions and exhortations to the faithful often assume that men and women today could spend as much time in prayer and worship as their forefathers, if they really wanted to do so. Actually most Christian intellectuals would like to give much more time to quiet reflection than they find possible. There is no easy solution of this problem; but just because the conditions are so adverse the good Christian intellectual will consider very seriously how he can make time for personal communion with God, by having a rule to spend so many minutes in prayer daily, by observing Sunday as a day of rest and worship, and by going away each year for a retreat of some days' duration.[1]

The intellectual should not be surprised if he finds prayer more difficult than most people do. For most people to turn aside in order to think and read and be quiet is in itself a rest and a refreshment. But the intellectual's main job is to think and read, though not always to be quiet! The point is that, unlike other people, when he prays he is using the same faculties that he is using all the time. Moreover, he is expected suddenly to turn round and to use them in an almost opposite manner. When he is not praying, he must use his mind to master his subject, he must be critical of everything that comes before him; but when he prays, he must submit his mind to be taught of God, he must listen like a child instead of laying down the law like a scholar or an expert. These are inevitable difficulties for the intellectual, and they have not yet been sufficiently reckoned with by those who offer guidance in the art of prayer.

[1] For more precise suggestions, see *Prayer for Busy People*, by John Townroe (S.P.C.K., 9d.).

No more than an earthly father, does God make himself known to his children according to general rules and regulations. God's dealings with every one of his children are unique, and we may be sure that he tenderly regards the peculiar difficulties of the intellectual who is in earnest.

THE GOOD CHRISTIAN INTELLECTUAL IS A LAY THEOLOGIAN

He does not leave theology to the professionals, but realizes that thinking out, and handing on, and applying the Christian faith is a task in which all Christians have their part to play, and that intellectuals have a special responsibility for it both because of their powers of thought and of their opportunity of helping and influencing others. This means too that he must bring the knowledge that he is acquiring in his own particular field of study or in his own section of human experience to the light of the revelation of God in Christ Jesus. He will not be content to keep his thinking in water-tight compartments, but will be trying to see everything and everybody in relation to the living God. This does not mean that he will try to force all knowledge into a logically compacted Christian system of thought. He will always respect the discipline and autonomy which are proper to each intellectual pursuit. But, while remaining aware that all human knowledge is compassed about with mystery and enigma, he will never be satisfied until he has learned how to glorify God with his intellect whatever the field of its exercise. Thus the more sure he is of God in Christ as the Lord of his existence, the more deliberately will he refuse all facile and premature solving of difficulties. Whenever he thinks he has got a question nicely and comfortably closed, he will not be surprised if the Holy Spirit opens it up again, and in so doing teaches him that there is for the intellectual a way of the cross which he must learn to follow to the end.

THE GOOD CHRISTIAN INTELLECTUAL IS A RECONCILER

He knows how little he yet knows of all that there is to be known, and therefore he will always be ready to learn from others. Moreover, he knows that the living God is speaking to all men, whether or not they listen and obey, and he can set no limit to what God may be designing to teach him through other people. It is his calling to recognize and acknowledge truth through whatever channel it comes. He will resist the absurd notion that his own system of thought is finally and exclusively true, and will always be seeking to enlarge and deepen his understanding by listening to what others have to say. He will be particularly eager to learn from sincere men who are opposed to him, for he will suspect that, whatever superstructure they have erected on it, they have at bottom got hold of some principle the truth of which it is blasphemy to deny.

It is in fact the work of the good Christian intellectual to bring men and principles into unity, to break down the barriers of misunderstanding between man-made systems and exclusive schools of thought, and never to abandon the path of reconciliation. The Church ought to be the place where the upholders of all true principles meet and are at home. Wherever this drawing men together in the truth which transcends their partial understandings of it is going on, there Christ is at work, even if he is not openly acknowledged, and he can be relied on to bless his poor intellectuals who are unremitting in this work. On the negative side, it means that the good Christian intellectual will avoid quick and harsh judgments, will abhor arrogance in himself more more than in anyone else, and will be an impossible person in any group which expects its members to follow a strict party line. He is tolerant not because he regards all opinions as doubtful, but because he is sure that God is at work in His world leading all men into the truth.

THE GOOD CHRISTIAN INTELLECTUAL IS A PASTOR

He cares more for persons than for ideas or parties or causes. He has constantly to be watching himself about this, for his capacity for abstract thought and his interest in classifying people as well as things are liable to make him blind to the primacy of the personal. But after all it is persons who matter in the end, who matter to God, and who should matter to him. There is no lack of good ideas in the world today, nor of organizations to propagate them, but there is a terrible lack of pastors, or of 'guides, philosophers and friends'. By pastors we mean men or women who care for other people as persons, and who are willing to put all their capacity for sympathy and understanding at the disposal of others not in order to control, dominate, regiment or patronize them, but in order to help them to solve their own problems and answer their own questions.

Ministering to the flock of Christ is a good work to which all Christians (and not only the ordained ministry) are called according to their opportunities, and intellectuals have gifts and opportunities for it which others lack. The flock of Christ embraces not only members of the Church or professing Christians but all mankind, and not least the scattered and lost sheep. Owing to the intellectual confusion of this age, the decay of traditional assurances, the perils and anxieties that beset all considering men, the sense of impasse which weighs upon all who have taken the measure of the blatant propaganda of conflicting ideologies, it is not in the least strange that there should be a very large number of men and women who are perplexed, frustrated, profoundly fearful. These are not the only scattered and lost sheep of Christ, but it is to these that Christian intellectuals owe a special ministry.

Everywhere the Good Shepherd wills to make use of under-shepherds, and here above all he wants under-shepherds who will lead and not drive, under-shepherds through whom he may know his sheep and they may know him. The good Christian intellectual will hardly be able to help here, unless he has himself experienced the perplexities and fears of the disillusioned, and has really had to struggle for his faith. Then he will know that what is demanded of him is not the lofty exposition of an intellectual panacea, but a lowly readiness to enter into the doubts of others and a desire to see them, not accept his point of view but, move towards the light from where they are and only by such steps as they can honestly take. This is to say that he is not a master who wants to gather a company of disciples round himself, not a pundit who airily or aggressively dictates solutions, but a pastor who is eager, wherever he is allowed and encouraged, to help men to find their own way through their own intellectual and personal problems.

Very often, however, a sense of sheer inability to help will come upon him, and this will send him to his prayers with a fresh urgency and compassion. Thus he has to learn that it is impossible to be a good pastor without being a strong intercessor. He has to learn the meaning and the cost of the ministry of intercession; no man can succour his brethren who is not himself being succoured by the High Priest of the race. It is only in Christ, the Head of humanity, that men can come home to God. In him men are already bound to each other and can succour each other. It is the pastor who daily identifies himself with the universal intercession of the great High Priest who will be most serviceable to the Good Shepherd who is always seeking his lost sheep.

This sketch of the good Christian intellectual is obviously an ideal; it amounts to a counsel of perfection. But it is by no means a mere ideal, having no relation to actual possibilities. On the contrary, we have known men and women who through the power of the Spirit have been enabled to manifest these characteristics to a wonderful degree. Are they not aims which everyone, to whom the word of wisdom or of knowledge has been given, must keep constantly in view if he is to practise the obedience of a Christian man and to fulfil the particular form of ministry to which he has been called in the Body of Christ?

INDEX

This b